Effectiveness of oral health promotion: a review

Dr E J Kay
Turner Dental School
University of Manchester

Professor David Locker
Community Dental Health Services
Research Unit
University of Toronto

HEA Project Team
Jane Meyrick
Antony Morgan

HEA Project Team
Jane Meyrick   Research Project Manager
Antony Morgan   Head of Monitoring and Effectiveness Research

Special thanks are due to Richard Watt and Catherine Stillman-Lowe for their commentaries.

In the same series:
Health promotion in older people for the prevention of coronary heart disease and stroke
Health promotion in childhood and young adolescence for the prevention of unintentional injuries
Effectiveness of video for health education: a review
Effectiveness of mental health promotion interventions: a review
Health promotion interventions to promote healthy eating in the general population: a review
Health promotion with young people for the prevention of substance misuse

Forthcoming topics:
Healthy eating targeted work

For further information, tel. 0171 413 2624
To place an order, contact Marston Book Services, tel. 01235 465 565

© Health Education Authority, 1997

ISBN 0 7521 1006 3

Health Education Authority
Trevelyan House
30 Great Peter Street
London SW1P 2HW

Designed by Edwin Belchamber
Typeset by Wayzgoose
Cover design by Raymond Loewy International Ltd
Printed in Great Britain

Contents

Acknowledgements

Professor Locker and Dr Kay would like to extend their thanks to their research teams for the meticulous and dedicated assistance which they lent to this review. They also wish to offer very grateful thanks to Miss Pam Brown who typed the text, tables and references so many times.

Foreword

At the present time, resources for dental services are coming under increasing pressure and scrutiny. The value of, and outcomes from, oral health promotion are also being increasingly challenged. This review of the effectiveness of oral health promotion is therefore welcome.

A systematic approach to identification of papers and quality grading has been conducted by the authors of the review, and this approach, which is championed by the Cochrane Collaboration, has clear benefits. In particular, the clear description and documentation of the methodology applied allows proper appraisal and limits biases, as clear reasons for inclusions and exclusions of papers are given.

Research in oral health promotion is problematical, however, because of the difficulties in defining clear outcome measures. New ideas and theories are constantly emerging and there is a need to develop agreed outcome measures to facilitate research and evaluation in this area.

In summary, this review provides a good source of reference for oral health promoters, and should be an important first port of call for anyone intending to undertake research in the field of oral health promotion.

Alan Lawrence and Derek Richards
Centre for Evidence-Based Dentistry, Oxford

Structure of the report

The report began with a foreword by Alan Lawrence and Derek Richards from the Centre for Evidence Based Dentistry, Oxford followed by commentaries by Catherine Stillman-Lowe, the HEA Oral Health Account Manager and Dr Richard Watt, a Senior Lecturer in Dental Public Health at University College London, about why the review was commissioned and a discussion of some of the issues raised by the authors about the research evidence presented.

The report is then divided into three main sections: executive summary; main report and technical appendices. The *executive summary* contains the main findings; summary of findings from each area reviewed; recommendations for action for purchasers, policymakers and research.

The *main report* begins by providing background details including the burden of oral ill health; the evidence reviewed; definitions used and scope of the review. The report then presents all of the studies reviewed, in detail, in Chapters 2 to 8 including previous reviews and the grey literature.

The *technical appendices* present full tables of the studies reviewed; details of the methodology used in the review and a list of all of the literature references.

Commentary

Dr Richard G. Watt, University College London

The need to demonstrate the effectiveness of interventions is now widely accepted within the NHS. The most appropriate methodology to assess effectiveness of interventions and the implications drawn from the results of effectiveness reviews are, however, still a matter of contention and debate.[1] This review of the effectiveness of oral health promotion provides some important information essential for the development of this emerging discipline. It therefore contributes to the results of the other published reviews of oral health promotion and should inform and facilitate the debate within the dental profession over the future development of oral health promotion.

Oral health promotion aims to increase the control of individuals and communities over their oral health. It involves members of those communities as well as a range of dental and non-dental personnel, and adopts a number of complementary approaches. As outlined in the Ottawa Charter these include building healthy public policy, creating supportive environments, strengthening community action, reorienting health services and developing personal skills.[2] Oral health promoters have however tended to concentrate on health education as their principal weapon against dental diseases. This is based on the fifth element of health promotion, that of developing personal skills. Such a narrow focus which fails to address the underlying determinants of oral health will be largely ineffective and may actually widen existing inequalities.[3]

This review has highlighted certain shortcomings of oral health promotion and has proposed a range of recommendations. However before purchasing decisions are made based upon these results, the findings of this review need to be placed within a wider context. Evaluation of the effectiveness of health promotion is a very different process from that required for assessing the effectiveness of clinical interventions.[4] This review has adopted largely a statistically based quantitative methodology to assess the effectiveness of a discipline principally developed from a social science philosophical base. Many health promotion experts have argued that quantitative scientific methods alone are not appropriate for the evaluation of the effectiveness of health promotion.[4][5] In addition, a significant proportion of the materials reviewed are conventional health education interventions many of which date back to the late 1970s and early 1980s. Since then the practice, quality and theory of oral health promotion has evolved considerably. Finally, as the authors have stated, many of the studies reviewed had a very poor evaluation design which limited their ability to assess the impact of interventions fully. The oral health promotion literature apparently lacks examples of high quality interventions that have been fully evaluated. A systematic review is only as good as the evaluation studies informing it.

The clear message of this review is that traditional dental health education has never been demonstrated to be effective. For example the review has highlighted that toothbrushing programmes in schools are ineffective at improving oral hygiene, that mass media campaigns are not effective in changing either oral health knowledge or behaviour and that interventions have not successfully tackled oral health inequalities.

Oral health promotion therefore faces certain key challenges. There is a need to develop practice beyond the largely ineffective confines of dental health education to a more innovative health promotion style of working. Such an approach should be designed to tackle the underlying determinants of oral health through collaborative and complementary working practices. The creation of supportive environments which facilitate sustained individual behaviour change and are more effective at tackling oral health inequalities should be the aim of future strategy development.

Another challenge presented by the review is the need for the development of valid, robust and appropriate methods of evaluation: both of individual programmes and overall strategies. To achieve this will require increased collaboration between practitioners and academics. It is critical that a combination of evaluation methods that give the best assessment of the full range of benefits and costs of oral health promotion is developed.[6] In addition the standardisation of evaluation measures should be a priority. This would enable meaningful comparisons to be made between different interventions.

This report has highlighted the limitations of what has been achieved so far. The majority of the interventions reviewed have had a narrow focus and have been poorly evaluated. There is a need for academics, practitioners and the public to work together to develop and implement comprehensive, innovative and high quality oral health promotion strategies. These should aim to bring about sustainable improvements in oral health. Robust and appropriate evaluation methods will form an integral part of these interventions. The results of such evaluations will provide a rich basis for designing effective oral health promotion in the future.

References

1. Speller, V, Learmonth, A and Harrison, D. The search for evidence of effective health promotion. *British Medical Journal* 1997; 315, 361-363.

2. World Health Organization. The Ottawa charter: principles for health promotion. Copenhagen: WHO Regional Office for Europe, 1986.

3. Schou, L and Wigh,t C. Does Dental Health Education Affect Inequalities in Dental Health? *Community Dental Health* 1994; **11**:97–100.

4. Health Education Board for Scotland. How effective are effectiveness reviews? *Health Education Journal* 1996; **55**:359–362.

5. Tones K. Health of the Nation: Two Token Cheers for Health Promotion? In Daly, B ed. *Building Healthy Alliances, Oral Health Promotion Research Group Conference Proceedings*. Rossendale: Bianchi Press, 1995; 31–37.

6. Tones, K. Evaluation Research – Issues and Practice. In Tones, K and Tilford, S eds. *Health Education: Effectiveness, Efficiency and Equity*. London: Chapman and Hall, 1994; 49–71.

Commentary

Catherine Stillman-Lowe, HEA Oral Health Programme Manager

'Oral health promotion is drinking in the last chance saloon'

These were the words used by a consultant in dental public health in a private meeting recently, who considered that commissioners could not continue to fund indefinitely – on the basis simply of inertia – 'tired old approaches to dental health education'.

How can this review help to remedy this situation? As part of the HEA's commitment to developing evidence based health promotion, this report pulls together the limited literature on dental health education/oral health promotion and provides recommendations for purchasers, providers and researchers. In short, with the other reviews already published in this area,[1][2][3] it provides an agenda for what should be a vigorous and well-informed debate about the way forward for oral health promotion in the twenty-first century.

The report presents some encouraging findings for those working in the field of oral health promotion: evidence concerning the effectiveness of interventions incorporating the use of fluoride is strong; and interventions designed to improve oral hygiene are effective even when very simple direct instruction is used. In addition, positive recommendations are made to strengthen the design of future studies, for example the development of standardised non-clinical indicators to measure the full range of oral health outcomes.

There are potential pitfalls for those seeking to interpret the results of this report, however, and the following points are designed to set the review into a context that reduces the chances of inappropriate interpretation of its findings, or subsequent ill-informed action:

- It may be tempting for hard-pressed purchasers reading this report to label particular types of intervention, such as attempts to reduce the amount and frequency of sugar consumption, to be 'proven to be ineffective', and therefore unworthy of further investment. However, definitive judgements should be resisted, given the limited literature available to the authors for inclusion, and the current methodological debate about systematic reviewing, as applied to health promotion.[4][5]

It could also be easy for the debate over what is effective in promoting oral health to focus largely upon individual approaches to disease prevention, and the relative priority of some of the messages set out in *The Scientific Basis of Dental Health Education*:[6] is oral hygiene more important than controlling the intake of sugar, in preventing dental caries, for example? Clarity of thought is not helped when there are powerful vested commercial interests involved in both producing oral hygiene products, and foods and drinks containing sugar.

We must be aware that the scarcity of evidence of effectiveness may simply reflect a tendency for national and local purchasers and providers of oral health promotion to channel funds purely into interventions, without investing in evaluation. Ultimately, this is self-defeating, as even if interventions are commissioned in the short-term, they cannot be demonstrated to be effective without appropriate evaluation, which in turn undercuts any rational argument for continuing to invest in the area in the future. The paucity of evidence available for inclusion in this report is a powerful argument for evaluation of oral health promotion initiatives to be commissioned and conducted to the highest quality standards, and published in peer-reviewed journals, whenever possible.

We should also consider that it may be the more innovative approaches to oral health promotion that are particularly vulnerable to inappropriate evaluation, or no evaluation at all. Measuring the costs and benefits of attempts to create a supportive environment for behavioural change is as yet an inexact science, and some well known oral health promotion activities, such as the recent campaign to remove sweets from supermarket checkouts, are not 'controlled' by any one agency, as participation is encouraged from a very wide range of individuals and organisations. Who could confidently assert what the total inputs and outputs of this initiative have been over the years, and thus assess whether or not it has been cost-effective?

Other legitimate factors in the purchasing equation should be considered, in addition to the results of systematic reviews. For example, a balance is needed between the good that an intervention may achieve, and the harm that it may inflict inadvertently. An inadequately researched campaign that adopts a 'victim-blaming' approach, and inspires guilt in its target audience but no positive action, is an example of a damaging health promotion intervention. Similarly, a campaign that creates a substantial demand for a screening service that is inadequately resourced to deal with the resulting flood of worried patients, could be counterproductive. Thus, the possible negative effects of any intervention, whether clinical or health promoting, should always be taken into account.

● Finally, we must be aware of our own values, as these too have a part to play in deciding what oral health promotion/dental health education services are purchased or provided. It may be regarded as an ethical duty by some to impart information on the causes of a disease, even if it is doubtful that as a result of this, behaviour will be modified and the prevalence reduced. Equally, it may be regarded by others as unethical to invest in an area of doubtful effectiveness, if by doing so interventions known to be effective are starved of resources.[7] If values are made explicit, they can at least be debated.

These barriers to appropriate action may seem many and formidable, but it is essential that readers of this report place the recommendations made into a broader context, as indicated by this and the external commentary provided, so that a valuable debate – and positive action – can result, and oral health promotion can confidently claim its place alongside the treatment and care services that have traditionally been the focus of NHS dentistry.

References

1. Brown, L F. Research in dental health education and health promotion: a review of the literature. *Health Education Quarterly* 1994; **21**(1):83–102.

2. Schou, L and Locker, D. Oral Health: A review of the effectiveness of health education and health promotion. IUHPE; 1994.

3. Sprod, A J, Anderson, R and Treasure, E T. *Effective Oral Health Promotion.* Health Promotion Wales; 1996.

4. Health Education Board for Scotland. How effective are effectiveness reviews? *Health Education Journal* 1996; **55**:359–62.

5. Speller, V, Learmonth, A and Harrison, D. The search for evidence of effective health promotion. *British Medical Journal* 1997; **315**:361–363.

6. Levine, R S, (ed). *The Scientific Basis of Dental Health Education.* Health Education Authority; 1996.

7. Kelly, M. *A Code of Ethics for Health Promotion.* The Social Affairs Unit; 1996.

Executive summary

Main findings

- Oral health promotion* which includes the use of therapeutic agents incorporating fluoride is effective in reducing the development of caries.† These improvements are cumulative and increase over time. There is no evidence of effectiveness of educative programmes aimed at caries reduction, if they do not involve the use of fluoride agents.

- School-based health education aimed at improving oral hygiene has not been shown to be effective. In contrast, clinical chairside interventions aimed at improving oral hygiene have been demonstrated to be effective.

- Oral health promotion aimed at improving oral hygiene is capable of reducing plaque levels. Simple approaches are as effective as more complex interventions but the changes brought about are difficult to sustain.

- The evidence reviewed suggests that oral health promotion is effective for increasing knowledge levels but a validated and standard instrument for the measurement of dental health knowledge is required if this is to be confirmed. However, there is no evidence that changes in knowledge are causally related to changes in behaviour.

- Although oral health promotion can increase levels of oral hygiene, the relationship between plaque control‡ and the health of the gingivae (gums) is not a simple one. Further research is necessary in order to clarify the multifactorial nature of gingivitis§ and periodontal (gum) diseases.¶

- Methods of measuring dental attitudes and beliefs in a meaningful, valid and standardised way are needed. Before such instruments are available, the effect of various oral health promotion efforts on attitudes will remain unclear.

*oral health promotion – 'any process which enables individuals or communities to increase control over the determinants of their oral health'.
†caries – tooth decay.
‡plaque – accumulations of microbiological flora on the teeth.
§gingivitis – reversible inflammation of the gum margins.
¶periodontal disease – non-reversible pathology of the structures supporting the teeth.

- Attempts to control individuals' consumption of sweet foods and drinks are generally not satisfactorily evaluated. However, when such interventions are directed towards individuals, they appear to be of limited value.

- 'Token economies' and other formalised reward and punishment regimes are effective for changing health-related behaviours in children. However, whether such changes are incorporated into a child's general lifestyle is not known. Interventions which use 'punishments' reduce, rather than enhance, choice and therefore cannot be recommended.

- There is no convincing evidence of the effectiveness of mass media programmes designed to promote oral health.

Summary of findings

Caries
Evidence concerning the effectiveness of the use of fluoride (whether in the form of toothpaste, tablets, drops, gels or rinses) and caries is strong. Thus, health promotion interventions which incorporate the regular use of one or other of these items are effective as long as compliance is achieved. Daily brushing with a fluoride toothpaste is easier to achieve than regular use of other fluoride supplements. There is no evidence that oral health promotion per se affects caries rates, even if changes in behaviour are achieved, unless fluoride is being used. There is also no available evidence that oral health promotion is able to affect dietary practices to an extent whereby caries levels are reduced. The most cost-effective means of delivering fluoride to the population should be the method of choice for promoting oral health through caries reduction.

Oral hygiene
Oral health promotion on an individual level is effective for reducing plaque levels. However, there is strong evidence that the changes achieved are short term and are not sustained. Interventions designed to improve oral hygiene are effective even when very simple direct instruction is used. Cognitive-behavioural techniques are not required in order to achieve changes in plaque levels.

Gingival health
Reduction in plaque levels almost always, but not invariably, leads to reductions in inflammation and bleeding of the gingivae. The lack of specificity of this relationship and the unknown long-term health consequences of gingivitis make evaluation of oral health promotion in this field very difficult.

Knowledge, attitudes, behaviours and beliefs
(a) Knowledge
Improving individuals' knowledge of dental health matters can be achieved through oral health promotion and oral health education.* The clinical, behavioural and health significance of these shifts in knowledge are unknown and there is some evidence that there are no consequences from improvements in knowledge. However, there would appear to be an ethical responsibility for scientific knowledge to be disseminated to the public, irrespective of what the population does with that knowledge. Many studies show that enhancement of knowledge can be quickly and easily achieved via educative programmes.

(b) Attitudes and beliefs
The alteration of attitudes and beliefs in order to promote health via an extremely heterogeneous collection of methods is possible. However, evidence that such changes lead to health benefit is not available.

(c) Behaviour
Since very few studies measure behaviour directly, it is difficult to evaluate the effect of oral health promotion on behaviour. Reported behaviour and behavioural intention can be altered and oral hygiene behaviour can be improved in the short term by simple educative interventions.

Sugar consumption
There are remarkably few evaluations of the effect of oral health promotion on sugar consumption and those which are available frequently use reported behaviour as the measurement instrument. Thus, evaluations of health promotion aimed at altering sugar consumption often describe changes in knowledge levels rather than altered habits or lifestyles.

Conclusions
Despite hundreds of studies involving thousands of individuals, we know remarkably little about how best to promote oral health. Sustained use of fluoride reduces caries and good oral hygiene promotes gum health and appears to be related to self-esteem. Daily thorough brushing with a fluoride toothpaste is an oral health-promoting behaviour and is an achievable goal. Manipulation of sugar consumption or other means of promoting oral health has not been proven to be effective.

Recommendations for action

Purchasers
● Caries preventive efforts should be focused on children as the

*oral health education – any learning activity which aims to improve individuals' knowledge, attitudes and skills relevant to their oral health needs.

benefits are cumulative. The use of fluoride in some form is recommended, particularly in toothpaste.

● Oral hygiene advice by dental professionals should be given to adults suffering from periodontal disease as substantial, clinically measurable health benefits can be achieved by this approach.

● Local campaigns should be directed at reinforcing daily brushing with fluoride toothpastes.

● Dental health education should be part of the school curriculum but should focus on improved knowledge as an outcome rather than on alterations in behaviour.

● Purchasing authorities should play an advocacy role in respect of fluoridation of water, salt or milk.

Policymakers

● Policymakers should ensure that oral health promotion (OHP) is targeted in areas of deprivation as untargeted OHP will widen the social gap further.

● Policymakers should be aware of the role of fluoride in caries prevention and should press for fluoridation of water supplies where disease levels are highest.

● Dental staff should be encouraged and trained to offer simple and appropriate oral health and hygiene advice to adults who have periodontal disease.

● Oral health promotion should be evidence based and training in evaluation should be provided to those in the field.

Research

● Multivariate analyses of interventions should be undertaken in order to identify the importance of each of the variables which might influence oral health.

● There is an urgent need for costs to be included in the evaluation of oral health promotion as research is required to guide purchasing decisions in order that health gain for communities is provided with the limited resources available.

● Further research into the role and importance of gingivitis in children is required.

- Research into the reasons why changes in behaviour are not maintained is required.

- Researchers must develop a policy regarding evaluation work and should develop and share measurement tools. Data collection should always include information about socio-demographic variables.

- A concerted effort must be made to evaluate community action and policy changes, in terms of health outcomes.

The objectives of the oral health strategy

Caries prevalence in children by the year 2003

Objective – 70% of 5-year-old children should have had no caries experience.

Baseline – Proportion of caries-free children ranged from 43% to 69%.

Objective – On average, 5-year-old children should have no more than one decayed, missing or filled primary tooth.

Baseline – dmft (number of decayed, missing and filled deciduous teeth) between 1.04 and 2.67.

Source: British Association for the Study of Community Dentistry. *The dental experience of 5-year-old children 1991/92.*

Objective – On average, 12-year-old children should have no more than one decayed, missing or filled permanent tooth.

Baseline – DMFT (number of decayed, missing or filled permanent teeth) of 1.2.

Source: *Child dental health survey 1993*, OPCS Monitor, table 2, February 1994

Periodontal diseases by the year 1998

Objective – The percentage of dentate adults over 45 years old with at least one deep periodontal pocket (greater than 6 mm) should be reduced to 10%.

Baseline – 17% of adults in the UK aged 45–54 had some deep pockets.

Source: *Adult dental health survey 1988*, table 13.1

Tooth loss in adults by the year 1998

Objective – 50% of 30-year-olds should have more than 20 teeth which are sound and unfilled.

Baselines – 23% of dentate adults in the UK aged 30 had more than 20 sound and untreated teeth in 1988.

– 63% of dentate adults in the UK aged 20 had more than 20 sound and untreated teeth in 1988.

Source: *Adult dental health survey 1988*, table 7.2

Objective – 75% of 50-year-olds should have more than 20 teeth.

Baseline – 60% of adults in the UK aged 45–54 had more than 20 teeth in 1988.

Source: *Adult dental health survey 1988*, table 4.2

Objective – 33% of adults over 75 years old should have teeth.

Baselines – 20% of adults in the UK aged over 75 had teeth in 1988.
– 63% of adults in the UK aged between 55 and 64 had teeth in 1988.

Source: *Adult dental health survey 1988*, table 4.2

Objective – 10% of adults over 75 years old should have more than 20 teeth.

Baselines – 3% of adults in the UK aged over 75 had more than 20 teeth in 1988.
– 11% of adults in the UK aged 65–74 had more than 20 teeth in 1988.

Source: *Adult dental health survey 1988*, table 4.2

1. Introduction

Context of the review

The review was commissioned by the Health Education Authority and was conducted in the Department of Oral Health and Development, University of Manchester, in collaboration with Professor David Locker of the University of Toronto in 1996. It provides a review of the research evidence on the effectiveness of health promotion aimed at improving oral health.

Oral health promotion interventions range from those aiming to create an (oral) health-promoting environment to those focusing on individual changes in knowledge, attitudes and/or behaviour. Thus, it has been hypothesised that oral health can be improved through health education, legislative and regulatory activities, fiscal change, community development, organisational change and the re-orientation of health services.[1] Efforts may also be directed towards reducing disease and injury to the teeth and their supporting structures/tissues, or may have as their aim promotion of feelings of wellbeing, speech and social acceptability.

The review therefore examines whether or not efforts to promote oral health are effective and if so what works best in what circumstances. However, it must be recognised that reviews are by nature retrospective. Thus, the work reviewed seldom reflects contemporary thinking about health, theories of behaviour or evaluation methodology.

Expectations and demands on dental services are likely to increase.[2] Estimates of the burden of oral disease are given in the Oral Health Strategy for England[3] along with target levels for reduction over the next decade. These are listed opposite.

Definitions

Oral health promotion – 'any process which enables individuals or communities to increase control over the determinants of their oral health'.

Oral health education – 'any learning activity which aims to improve individuals' knowledge, attitudes and skills relevant to their oral health'.

Caries – tooth decay.

DMFT – number of decayed, missing or filled permanent teeth.

dmft – number of decayed, missing or filled deciduous teeth.

Periodontal disease – non-reversible pathology of the structures supporting the teeth.

Gingivitis – reversible inflammation of the gum margins.

Plaque – accumulations of microbiological flora on the teeth.

The burden of oral ill health

Oral health is a term which refers to much more than the simple possession of natural healthy teeth. Although disorders of the teeth and oral cavity are only rarely fatal, they are a common cause of pain[4][5] and an important source of disability and handicap. Poor oral health limits personal choices and social opportunities and diminishes life satisfaction in the same way as diseases of other body systems.[6][7]

The accepted definition of oral health is 'a standard of health of the oral and related tissues which enables an individual to speak and socialise without active disease, discomfort or embarrassment and which contributes to general wellbeing'. This broad definition of oral health makes the burden of oral health in terms of suffering and social cost almost impossible to quantify but at least £1.5 billion of NHS funding is used directly in dental care[8] and these costs are set to rise as older people make up a greater proportion of the population and more people retain their teeth into later life.

Although the dental and oral health of the UK population has improved significantly over the last twenty years, many challenges remain. As levels of health have improved, inequities have widened and functional and psychosocial problems associated with poor oral health are particularly marked in already vulnerable populations such as the elderly and low-income groups. In the UK, poor oral health is becoming a characteristic of the socially disadvantaged and the elderly.

In the post-war years, the oral health of the nation was poor and NHS dental services were faced with enormous demand for both surgical and restorative treatments. However, because of the improvements which have taken place, it is now possible for oral health care policy to focus more fully on the prevention and early detection of oral ill health. However, unlike some of the analogous medical services, oral health care services have always considered dental health education and (to a lesser degree) oral health promotion to be important and an integral part of the care offered to the population. Levels of knowledge, attitudes, intentions, beliefs, behaviours, use of services and oral health status have all been targeted for change and these efforts are perhaps testimony to dentistry's long-standing concern with the prevention of oral disease via the adoption of healthier life practices.

It has long been presumed that such efforts will reduce disease and thus lower the demand for health services and the resultant costs. This report attempts to collate the scientific evidence underlying this assumption and aims to provide a systematic overview of what is worth doing to promote oral health and what works best under which circumstances.

The evidence reviewed

The review involved computerised searching of five electronic databases, systematic handsearching of 94 scientific journals, plus personal contacts with experts and practitioners. In total, 192 papers were retrieved. Of these, 28 were descriptive or theoretical but did not describe evaluation of an oral health promotion initiative and one was a simple case study. They were therefore excluded. Thus, overall, 163 papers relevant to the review were critically appraised. The literature was categorised by outcome measure, and the methodology, population group, setting and quality of the study were recorded. Quality measures applicable to all intervention studies of whatever design were used in order that quasi-experimental or time-series studies of high quality could be accorded as much weight as low quality studies with more rigorous study designs. In total, 36 randomised control trials, 80 quasi-experimental studies and 33 single group studies were identified. In addition, 7 multiple baseline studies and 8 descriptions of mass media oral health promotion programmes were included in the review. Single papers often described multiple experiments focusing on several different outcomes. These were considered separately and each part of the experiment was described and analysed according to the outcome measure. The review includes both quantitative and qualitative analyses and these are presented in Chapters 4–9. The review includes quantitative meta-analysis where appropriate and qualitative syntheses of the data where quantitative methodologies were deemed unsuitable.

Quantitative synthesis of the evidence was carried out for papers which included sufficient data and which reported randomised controlled trials of an intervention. Statistical techniques were used to pool the data from similar studies and thus an overall intervention effect could be calculated.

For studies which did not report sufficient data to include them in the formal meta-analysis, qualitative synthesis of the results was undertaken. This synthesis used the following rationale in order to draw conclusions:

If the majority of studies within each methodological group showed an outcome effect, the conclusion was drawn that there was robust evidence of a strong effect which was not masked by poor research design or small numbers of participants. If, however, the majority of studies in each methodological group showed no intervention effect, then the conclusion drawn was that there was no evidence that oral health promotion was effective.

If the majority of studies with randomised controlled trials or quasi-experimental designs showed an effect on an outcome, while the majority of studies with less acceptable research designs showed no effect, the conclusion was drawn that the intervention effect was real but small. Interventions with only small effects on the outcome will not be revealed by studies of poor design or low power (β error).

If the majority of studies with strong research designs showed no intervention effect and less well-designed studies showed a positive effect, the conclusion was drawn that no real effect existed and that α-error and biases introduced by poor design had led to false results.

Scope of the review

The broad scope of the term oral health promotion makes it difficult to define the precise outcomes which are to be achieved by the activity. This review assumed that the promotion of knowledge is as valid an objective as changes in disease status, and thus all retrievable evaluative studies purporting to influence oral health in any way were included in the review. What the review does not include is theoretical models or reviews of methodologies. It also does not include health promotion directed towards smoking cessation as this issue will be covered in other reviews. It concentrates on the changes which can be brought about by oral health promotion interventions and seeks to identify what works best, in what circumstances and with whom involved.

The review includes studies of efforts made to enhance the oral wellbeing of the population. It did not include interventions which rely solely on the delivery of a therapeutic agent but is limited to studies where knowledge and an activity or behaviour must be used by an individual to enhance the health of either themselves, or another person or population. Thus, toothpaste trials and fluoridation studies are excluded – unless they involve active participation and behaviour change in one or more people. The review covers randomised controlled trials, quasi-experimental design studies (studies which included a comparison group), single group before-and-after studies, studies with multiple baseline designs and mass media programmes. Finally, the findings of previous reviews are documented.

For each outcome measure, the findings are grouped according to the design of the studies involved. Details regarding the target population and settings are given in the tables. Diverse study designs and multiple outcomes were covered in the review. In order that the most reliable information could be accorded greater weight, a measure of quality was applied to each study. The scoring system is fully described in Appendix C. The quality scores achieved by each study is indicated in the tables and is taken into account in the qualitative summations of the evidence, according to the rationale described on p.10.

The results are described in Chapters 3–7, each detailing the findings for a particular outcome measure. It should be noted that multiple interventions may be discussed in more than one section and may be deemed to have been effective for one type of outcome, yet ineffective for another.

2. Types of studies reviewed

Randomised controlled trials

The randomised controlled trial (RCT) is considered to be the 'gold-standard' evaluation methodology. Such studies involve random allocation of participants to test and control groups and blind assessment of the study outcome measure. Unfortunately, oral health promotion does not lend itself easily to such a study design and even when the methodology is used, it is frequently inadequately applied. In particular, randomisation to treatment and control group is often poor and it is very difficult to achieve double-blinding if the intervention requires the participating individuals to undertake an activity. The threats to validity and biases introduced by failing to use such an RCT design are well recognised but are discussed in Appendix B. However, a poorly conducted RCT may well give less reliable evidence than a well-conducted study with a different design. Thus, whilst the studies detailed in the RCT sections might be considered to offer the most robust evidence, the quality scores must be taken into consideration when drawing conclusions from the results of these studies. Some of the RCTs were of poorer quality than the studies detailed in later sections.

Quasi-experimental studies

These studies were designed with a comparison group of similar nature. The results of these studies cannot in general be considered to be as robust as the results of the studies with an RCT design. However, many of the evaluations detailed had acceptable study designs which can probably be relied on. It can be seen that these quasi-experimental studies can be considered to offer much more substantial evidence than those with single group designs but once again the quality of the study and the reporting are reflected in the quality scores shown in the tables. Those with higher quality scores should be considered to offer the more reliable results.

Single group studies

These sections synthesise the results of a number of studies which used a pre-/post-test evaluation design. This study design is not generally considered to be robust (see Appendix B) as the lack of control group leaves it open to many potential threats to the validity of the findings. However, if the study is well conducted and reported, the simplicity of the design allows easy interpretation of the results. A common flaw among the studies reported in these sections was incomplete reporting of both baseline and follow-up data. Also, the length of time between the intervention and data collection was repeatedly not reported. Thus, for a sizeable proportion of these studies, no firm conclusions can be legitimately drawn.

Multiple baseline studies

This section, found only in Chapter 4, discusses a number of studies which do not fit into any of the other major categories of study design. The studies are included because they demonstrate novel approaches to both health promotion and data collection. It may be that these studies reflect the 'real world' more adequately than those previously described because they concentrate on individuals rather than groups. The RCT, quasi-experimental and single group studies attempt to control or account for the variables affecting individuals' behaviours. However, such designs also raise ethical questions concerning the withholding of treatment from control groups and the lack of homogeneity among the participants, i.e. those studies cannot adequately take account of atypical behaviours. Multiple baseline studies do not use mean scores but compare each individual or group with another, using individual scores for the changes which take place subsequent to an observation.

3. Interventions aimed at reducing caries

Randomised controlled trials
– caries (*N* = 7) Table 3.1

In general, the studies which examined the effects of health promotion on caries levels[9–15] focused upon reducing caries by improving oral hygiene through active participation, education or enforcement of brushing regimes in schools. The majority of these studies report small non-significant effects on caries increment although in many the follow-up period was too short to expect measurable differences to be observed. More importantly, almost all interventions which used caries levels as an outcome measure involved some type of professional prophylaxis and the administration of fluoride in tablets, rinses or toothpaste. It is therefore impossible to determine whether the educative intervention, the effect of professional ministrations or the therapeutic action of fluoride caused the observed reductions in caries increments. The reduction in caries by a mean of 1.8 surfaces (95% CI 0.384, 3.264) suggests that interventions involving professional staff and regular prophylaxis do have an effective role. However, costs are not reported in any of the literature. Such programmes also offer the greatest benefits to those who least need it, i.e. those with the lowest levels of disease. Further research is required in order to separate the effects of education, fluoride and professional time and there is a pressing need for studies to be costed in order to identify the most cost-effective means of reducing caries. If caries reduction alone is considered, professionally based programmes would not provide a more cost-effective means of lowering caries rates than fluoridation of water supplies.

Quasi-experimental studies
– (caries) (*N* = 11) Table 3.2

The quasi-experimental studies which stated caries reduction as one of the aims of the intervention[16–26] show that, if the intervention involved daily toothbrushing with a fluoridated toothpaste, caries could be reduced. However, the size of the intervention effect was dependent on the length of the follow-up, with greater reductions being observed with long-term follow-up. No study with a follow-up period of 6 months or less demonstrated any measurable effect on caries rates.

For interventions which did not involve daily brushing but relied more heavily on educative components, there was no evidence that caries levels were affected (Table 3.2).

Single group studies
– caries (*N* = 3) Table 3.3

Only three pre-/post-test studies[27][28][29] purported to investigate the effectiveness of the intervention on caries levels. In one of these[27] in which parents were educated about the oral care of their children, the intervention appeared to be effective. In contrast, the design and reporting of the other two studies in this category failed to present results which allow any conclusions about effectiveness to be drawn.

4. Interventions aimed at improving oral hygiene

Randomised controlled trials
– oral hygiene (*N* = 23) Table 4.1

The vast majority of the studies classified as randomised controlled trials[11][13][30–50] used the plaque levels in the participants' mouths as one of their outcome measures. Unfortunately, not all studies measured the plaque in the same way. In general, studies demonstrated that oral hygiene can be improved in most people but changes are not sustained. The conclusions drawn in each study therefore vary, depending on the length of the follow-up period. Studies with short follow-up periods more often showed significant improvements in plaque levels, whilst studies with long periods of follow-up more often suggested that instruction and education were not effective in the long term.

A further conclusion which can be drawn from these studies is that an intervention aimed at improving oral hygiene is likely to lead to small short-term reductions in plaque levels and this effect is independent of the method used, i.e. dental health education can change people's behaviours and the more elaborate and theoretically based interventions appear to be no more successful than simple ones. There was one notable exception. Alcouff's study[37] in which individuals were interviewed for an hour by a psychologist showed a significant and lasting effect on plaque levels (18.7% reduction in plaque scores). However, the efficiency of such a technique must be called into question, except perhaps for the most disease-prone individuals. Table 4.1 shows the RCTs directed at plaque reduction.

Statistical meta-analysis of the studies which used the plaque index as an outcome measure and gave sufficient statistical information showed that the mean effect was a 0.316 reduction in the plaque index (95% CI −0.063, 0.695), i.e. 32% less tooth surfaces are covered by plaque subsequent to an intervention. However, because of the inclusion of zero in the confidence interval, it must be concluded that oral hygiene is not reliably improved by the interventions described in Table 4.1.

Quasi-experimental studies
– oral hygiene (*N* = 36) Table 4.2

The vast majority of the quasi-experimental interventions aimed at improving oral hygiene were carried out in schools or dental clinics.[22] [51–85]

A number of conclusions can be drawn from the data, although an overall intervention effect cannot be calculated due to the diversity of the study methods and insufficiencies in the data.

There is no evidence that school-based educative programmes have any effect on the plaque levels of the participants, even if daily brushing at school is part of the programme. Indeed, school-based programmes, whether run by dental professional, teacher, or by older pupils teaching younger, were never demonstrated to affect oral hygiene.

The clinic-based interventions gave extremely variable results. Some studies showed dramatic reductions in plaque levels in people who had been exposed to an experimental programme. What is interesting is that these results seemed to be independent of the methods used in the intervention. This would suggest that this is an 'operator' effect and this view is supported by the fact that when successful strategies for inducing plaque control are transferred from one clinic to another, results are often not maintained.

The few community-based studies available suggest that the most successful interventions are those which are targeted at very young children and include home visits. Educating parents about plaque control in their offspring is effective.

Single group studies
– oral hygiene (*N* = 21) Table 4.3

As for the previous studies described, the conclusion which could be drawn from the single group studies[52] [86] [88–107] is that most interventions were successful in reducing the plaque levels in the mouths of the participants. The reductions were of the order of 30%, i.e. plaque control interventions can improve oral cleanliness by approximately one-third. This order of reduction appears to be independent of the setting, target group or detail of the intervention. Two provisos must be made about this finding. Firstly, many of the studies had very short follow-up periods and thus, although improvements are seen, this does not imply that they will be sustained. Secondly, given the multifactorial nature of the relationship between plaque levels and disease, it is not possible to draw conclusions about the long-term clinical significance of these plaque reductions. That is, a 30% decrease in the amount of plaque in a person's mouth may, or may not, have a significant effect on the clinical health status of that person.

Multiple baseline studies
– oral hygiene (*N* = 7)

One interesting study[108] demonstrated that four times more children achieved adequate plaque control after pictures of them were posted in the classroom. This intervention was deemed to have been more effective than preceding education, feedback, instruction and praise and encouragement. Only the children who brushed effectively had their pictures posted. However, this study raises questions regarding victim blaming and punishment as means of inducing health-related behaviour and this approach cannot thus be recommended.

Other studies[109] have used token economies, whereby children are rewarded with stars or money for undertaking adequate oral hygiene behaviours. Shifting criteria for earning tokens ensured continued improvements in the children's plaque control. Such individually-specific designs may be helpful but cannot be recommended due to the expense of designing and maintaining programmes for each child. Simplified versions of token economies applied to groups have not been shown to be effective.

A further study[110] showed that prompts and rewards were not effective for improving flossing behaviour. The study demonstrated that, although children will report increased frequency of oral hygiene behaviours, the adequacy with which the behaviour is performed means that no improvements in plaque control are achieved. Since flossing has not been proven to be an effective means of reducing disease, encouragement of the behaviour cannot be condoned.

Swin, Allard and Holborn[111] introduced a 'Good Toothbrushing Game' as a school-based programme. The success of the game was measured by scoring the oral hygiene of selected 'team' members each day. Winning teams were rewarded with stickers and having their names posted. This regime brought about improved oral hygiene. This use of peer pressure and reward is an interesting concept but further research into the overall effects of such methods on children's psychological welfare should be carried out before similar programmes could be recommended for use generally.

Other investigators[112 113] have used multiple baseline across subjects with reward and feedback to improve flossing and toothbrushing. However, the complex and expensive nature of the study design, reward systems and the small numbers of children involved mean that these studies are of academic rather than practical use.

One multiple baseline study[114] involved adults and, although the intervention successfully reduced plaque levels, the improvements were not maintained. This finding concurs with the conclusions drawn in previous sections of this chapter. Further research about the process of relapse should be undertaken as it has important implications for oral health promotion programmes.

5. Interventions aimed at improving gingival health

Randomised controlled trials
– gingival health (*N* = 11) Table 5.1

Gingival health can be measured using a number of indices. Bleeding of the gingivae on probing and probing depth are two common outcome measures used in such studies.[9 13 34 41 42 43 47 49 115 116 117] Such measures are, however, notoriously subjective and operator dependent. Similarly, the exact meaning of the measures in terms of oral health is not clear. Bleeding on probing is assumed to be a measure of inflammation which is caused by plaque accumulation. However, individual responses to microbial challenges are notoriously idiosyncratic and thus the use of this index for measuring oral ill health must be called into question. Similarly, probing depths, whilst being a useful measure of past disease, are now generally accepted to be unrelated to current or future disease status.

Overall, the evidence suggests that if a programme is successful in reducing plaque levels, then some improvement in gingival health (as measured by bleeding on probing and probing depth) can be expected. However, the studies reported show that plaque reductions are not reliably achieved, particularly in the long term, and, even if they are, this does not always lead to improved gingival health. Whether these observations are due to flaws in experimental design, the indices used or true lack of effectiveness cannot be conclusively drawn from the studies described in Table 5.1. Further research into the indices and the links between plaque, inflammation and disease is required.

Quasi-experimental studies
– gingival health (*N* = 21) Table 5.2

In general, the results of these studies[12 18 19 23 25 41 58 59 60 62 63 65 69 70 73 77 118 119 120 121 122] indicated that clinic-based plaque control programmes are generally effective and that they can improve gingival and periodontal health. In contrast, there is little evidence to suggest that programmes in schools aiming at improving gingival health are effective.

This finding is of importance since professional clinic-based time is expensive. If they were as effective as clinic-based programmes, the use of school time to undertake plaque and gingivitis control programmes would be appealing in terms of cost benefit ratios. However, since there is no evidence that such regimes confer advantages on the participants, periodontal health should remain under the jurisdiction of preventive dental services.

The finding that clinic-based programmes are effective, regardless of the type of intervention, suggests that professional time, particularly that of hygienists, has a large contribution to make towards oral health gain.

Single group studies
– gingival health (*N* = 8) Table 5.3

Synthesis of the results of these studies[28] [89] [90] [123–127] leads to an equivocal conclusion. In studies involving children, where sufficient interpretable data are presented, the interventions seemed to give some reduction in gingival inflammation but the changes are small and, as stated in previous chapters, such measurements suffer from a degree of lack of objectivity. In contrast, for adult patients who are already suffering from periodontal disease, the evidence suggests that education and treatment from a hygienist can give important improvements in pocket depths.

6. Studies aimed at improving knowledge, attitudes, beliefs and behaviours

Randomised controlled trials
– knowledge (*N* = 7) Table 6.1

Many of the RCT studies[13][15][38][45][128][129][130] stated that improvement in knowledge was an aim of the intervention. However, the measurement and reporting of the extent to which this particular aim was achieved was very variable. A major problem exists when trying to draw conclusions from the data, namely that there is no agreed set of facts which 'should' be known and no agreed way of measuring such knowledge. Thus, each study uses ad hoc knowledge scales and often little detail is reported. It is therefore impossible to determine the 'comparability' of these studies, or to pool the data. What emerges from the knowledge studies is however a universal conclusion that knowledge levels can be improved and that this is relatively easy to do. It would also seem that complex or highly technical educative methods add little benefit. Thus, the simple provision of information is adequate if knowledge is the outcome of interest. Having said this, a number of the studies point out that translating improvements in knowledge into changes in behaviour is much more difficult to achieve. Indeed, the studies which measured both knowledge and behaviour gave a consensus view that few differences in behaviour could be attributed to changes in knowledge. RCT studies which aimed to improve knowledge are listed in Table 6.1.

– attitudes, beliefs and behaviours (*N* = 11) Table 6.2

The studies,[15][45][50][116][119][129][130][132][133][134] which focused upon changing attitudes towards, and beliefs about, oral health, used heterogeneous methodologies and a number of ad hoc scales. Whilst these scales are possibly valid indicators of oral health intentions, their ad hoc use and lack of uniformity, along with the low level of detail given in the papers, make the results difficult to interpret. However, as with the studies which aimed to improve knowledge, the consensus is that oral health promotion efforts are almost invariably successful in altering reported attitudes and beliefs but that these changes do not necessarily lead to alterations in behaviour. The changes which can be achieved seem to be a result of the intervention regardless of the method used, for example, instruction is as effective as cognitive-behavioural therapy. Also, the changes seem to be short-lived, although conclusive proof of this conjecture is unavailable due to the lack of uniformity of follow-up period (Table 6.2).

Quasi-experimental studies
– knowledge (*N* = 14) Table 6.3

Of the quasi-experimental studies which aimed to improve the participants' levels of knowledge,[58 69 77 78 80 81 84 135–141] only a very small minority failed to show that this could be achieved. Almost all of the evaluations measured substantial improvements in knowledge. The school setting was unsurprisingly the one most often used for these educative interventions, although two studies which took place in the workplace also demonstrated substantial improvements in the knowledge levels of the intervention group.

Thus, it can be concluded that dental health education is effective in bringing about improvements in knowledge. However, it must be noted that the extent to which high levels of knowledge affect either attitudes or behaviour or, ultimately health, remains unclear.

Furthermore, there is as yet no universal agreement regarding what is 'dental knowledge'. Thus, there is no common aim shared by the studies reported and the results are not directly comparable because no single validated instrument is used to assess their effect. There is an urgent need for researchers to try to make their results generalisable by using standard measures. Although the studies reviewed indicate that it is certainly an achievable aim to increase the levels of dental knowledge in a population, it is impossible to know which methods or settings work best, since the results of one individual study cannot be directly compared with that of another.

– attitudes, beliefs (*N* = 16) Table 6.4

The effect of oral health promotion on attitudes and beliefs is much less clear cut than the effects on knowledge.[56 69 77 78 80 81 84 135 137 138 139 142–145] About half of the studies reported that oral health promotion had had a positive effect on attitudes and beliefs. However, the significance of these reported findings is difficult to assess. The measures used were often poorly reported, or not reported at all. Secondly, many used ad hoc scales, the responses to which may or may not be meaningful and may or may not have a significant bearing on health behaviours. The variance in the results may therefore have as much to do with the validity of the measurement instruments as with the effectiveness of the interventions. The development and universal use of a dental attitudes and beliefs scale would make an important contribution to a researcher's ability to adequately evaluate the effectiveness of interventions aimed at influencing attitudes.

Quasi-experimental studies
– behaviour (*N* = 13) Table 6.5

A number of studies[17 77 78 82 135 137 140 146-151] stated that the aim of the intervention was to influence or alter the behaviour of the participants. Behaviour is, however, notoriously difficult to measure and reported behaviour, or reported behavioural intention, are inadequate substitutes. This problem results in the evaluations' failing to present results relating to behaviour. Thus it is difficult to draw conclusions from the studies reviewed. It would appear that, subsequent to an intervention, people report that they brush their teeth more frequently and one study demonstrated that children's food choices can be influenced by dental health programmes in schools. However, these conclusions are highly speculative and the weight and quality of the evidence cannot be said to suggest that oral health promotion is effective in influencing oral health behaviour.

Single group studies
– knowledge (*N* = 10) Table 6.6

The 'knowledge studies' with pre-/post-test designs were often reported in a way which makes synthesis of the results extremely difficult.[52 97 99 102 105 106 128 152-154] Differences in proportions of individuals answering a particular question correctly do not indicate an increase in general dental health knowledge. However, the use of overall scores for knowledge tests is also rather unhelpful, as the representativeness and validity of the questions asked are unknown. In general, participants seemed to know more after an intervention than they did before the experiment. Whether this finding is evidence of the effectiveness of oral health promotion must remain open to question. The lack of validated research tools for use in this field is a major problem.

Single group studies
– attitudes and behaviours (*N* = 9)

The heterogeneity of the results reported in the studies in this section[154-162] makes synthesis impossible. No conclusions can be drawn regarding the effectiveness of these oral health promotion interventions aimed at altering attitudes, beliefs or behaviours.

7. Interventions aimed at altering sugar intake

Randomised controlled trials (*N* = 1)

Only one study with an RCT type of design focused on limitation of sugar intake.[163] In this interesting study, leaflets were distributed to pharmacists, informing them about the benefits of sugar-free medicines and providing a list of common OTC medicines for which there was a sugar-free alternative. The success of the promotion was measured by determining the level of stocking of sugar-free medicines and the extent to which pharmacists were recommending them. After 12 weeks, there was a clear increase in the number of recommendations made for sugar-free products.

This innovative study demonstrates a new and useful approach to oral health promotion which suggests that it may be useful to direct efforts and interventions towards the gatekeepers of information and products. In particular, if they are a profession who are traditionally expected to 'guide' the public, their influence on individuals' choices can be exploited to the benefit of the recipient population.

Quasi-experimental and single group studies (*N* = 47) Tables 7.1 and 7.2

Sugar eating behaviour suffers from the measurement difficulties cited in Chapter 6 and thus evaluation of the effectiveness of intervention is difficult.[14 77 78 148 152 164 165] Often, only reported behaviour is measured and this may not accurately reflect the actual behaviour of the individual. Only four studies[166–169] aimed to investigate the effect of oral health promotion on actual sugar consumption. Of these, three suggested that consumption of sweet food and drinks might be limited as a result of the intervention. However, given the sparsity of the data, this conclusion is highly speculative.

8. Mass media dental health campaigns

As documented earlier in this review, much oral health promotion is carried out by general dental practitioners in the clinical setting or in schools, using either dental professionals or teachers as the 'gatekeepers' of the information. Less frequently, community-based action involving home visits is used, particularly with parents of young children. Whilst these activities are sometimes effective, a different approach is to provide mass campaigns which reach large numbers of people. Such campaigns can be considered inexpensive in terms of the numbers of people reached but their effectiveness as a health-promoting device is questionable. This section briefly describes eight reports of mass media campaigns.

The 1979 Minnesota Dental Association Campaign focused on periodontal disease[170][171] and was evaluated by conducting personal interviews with 1000 individuals. This showed that 79% of the population were aware of the campaign and of these, 90% could correctly recall the message content. Ten per cent of the people who had seen the television advert reported that they intended to make more preventive dental visits in the future. However, the evaluation study did not determine the actual increase in demand for dental care and thus the effectiveness of the campaign in changing health-related behaviour is unknown.

A massive campaign is run in China each year, known as Love Teeth Day (LTD) which involves use of mass media (radio, television and newspapers) plus lectures, posters and pamphlets. The theme differs slightly each year. In 1992, the campaign was evaluated.[172] The LTD was reported to have reached 600 million people (54% of the Chinese population) in 1992. Questionnaire evaluation showed that knowledge levels, toothbrushing and use of dental care services have increased in the four years over which the campaigns have been run. This has been regarded as a success for the campaign. However, the evaluation methodology was insufficient and any improvements may have been incidental to the running of the programme.

Finland has also run a national campaign, aimed at encouraging the use of dental services, which was evaluated by interviewing 694 individuals. The campaign informed the public via mass media communication.

However, the evaluation interview did not ask the respondents about the campaign but only about their dental visiting habits and how dental disease could be prevented.[173] As in the Chinese study, changes across time were attributed to the campaign but no evidence was presented to substantiate this claim, except that the respondents felt that it was possible to keep their teeth for life (this was in keeping with the campaign's aim). In a separate evaluation survey only 49% of the population interviewed could recall the campaign message. It would therefore seem that the population's beliefs existed independently from the campaign.

A Norwegian evaluation of a national mass media campaign[174] showed that only 20% of the population interviewed could recall having seen the campaign motif. The majority (59%) of the respondents thought that campaigns were ineffective and 37% stated that they had no interest in such campaigns. It was concluded that no changes in behaviour could be ascribed to the campaign but it was suggested that the campaign created a 'preparedness' for later exposure to dental health messages.

A further report of the Norwegian campaign[175] showed that there had been no increase in knowledge as a result of the campaign. It was suggested that the role of mass communication is one of reinforcing existing beliefs rather than promoting knowledge or changing behaviour. Mass media campaigns are expensive and this raises a question regarding their suitability and cost-effectiveness if they are used only to reinforce existing beliefs.

Lastly, a study in Scotland[176] showed that a campaign using television advertising, women's magazines and schools was not well remembered. The school-based part of the programme had the most significant impact because it involved active participation. However, the study did not reveal any demonstrable changes in health or health-related behaviour.

In general, this review of mass media campaigns suggests that they are ineffective for promoting either knowledge or behaviour change. It is possible, though not proven, that they stimulate awareness. However, the body of evaluative research in the area is small, although much has been written on the theory of mass communication. The methodologies used in these evaluation studies are inadequate and thus no specific conclusions about the role of mass media can be drawn. In contrast, small-scale campaigns, such as one conducted inexpensively in a shopping centre, have been demonstrated to influence dental visiting behaviour.[177] In conclusion, there is no evidence that mass media campaigns succeed in promoting health. There is some evidence that local campaigns, which have an active involvement component, may have a role in promoting awareness.

It could be argued that the improvements in dental health which have been witnessed over the past thirty years have been due to product marketing by the manufacturers of dental health products – in particular fluoride toothpaste. When daily toothbrushing using such a product is adopted by increased numbers of individuals, both the manufacturers and consumers benefit. In 1990, the toothpaste industry was estimated to have spent £20 million on advertising campaigns. There is little question whether or not this alters the behaviour of the consumer – if it did not, the money would not be spent. Thus, whilst toothpaste manufacturers tend to focus their attention on the cosmetic attributes of oral hygiene, the behaviour encouraged does have a health benefit. Thus, it would seem that expensive media advertising can be assumed to be effective. Studies should be conducted to confirm this hypothesis.

9. Previous literature reviews

Four substantial reviews of oral health promotion have been published recently. One, commissioned by the Dutch Centre for Health Promotion and Health Education selected fourteen published studies.[178] The authors purposely included studies which were innovative in terms of their setting or target group. The review therefore included studies whose evaluative methodology was weak. Due to the non-systematic selection of papers for inclusion, the review is not representative of oral health promotion work as a whole and does not claim to be.

The review concluded that knowledge can be influenced by health education programmes, as can oral hygiene and reported eating habits. The review revealed that these improvements can be achieved in both elderly, adult and child population groups.

Some particularly interesting and innovative papers were included in the review. These are highlighted here, as they were not captured by the data search in the current review. One paper described education given to water treatment plant operators.[179] Subsequent to the intervention, there was a threefold increase in the number of water facilities which had water samples within the legal range.

This paper falls outside the traditional concept of health education and within the concept of health protection. It is surprising and perhaps disappointing that so few studies investigate alternative methods of promoting the health of the population.

Schou and Locker's review also examined two case studies which described efforts to influence decision-makers in ways which might promote the oral health of a population. One such paper examined strategies for achieving political support for water fluoridation[180] while another described a community development approach to reorganising dental services for the benefit of the local community.[181]

The conclusion which Schou and Locker drew from their selected papers was that traditional educational interventions can be effective. However, they also concluded that comprehensive strategies using programmes tailored to individual needs have greater effects and may lead to longer-term change.

The authors of the current work previously undertook a systematic review of the effectiveness of dental health education.[182] A total of 143 papers were retrieved but half were excluded due to poor study design and further studies were left out of the meta-analysis subsequent to validity checking. This work focused on the quality of the primary evaluations and combined quantitative and qualitative meta-analysis to draw the conclusion that dental health education has a small positive but temporary effect on plaque accumulation (reduction in plaque index 0.37) no discernible effect on caries increment, and a consistent positive effect on knowledge.

The authors conclude that the most successful oral health interventions are time- and labour-intensive and therefore likely to be costly but that health professionals have an ethical responsibility to disseminate information.

The most recent and comprehensive review of the literature was commissioned by Health Promotion Wales.[183] In a systematic review of medical, dental and social science literature, quality criteria were applied to the evaluation literature. This very detailed review divides papers according to the strength of the evidence offered by them and concludes that there is clear evidence that oral health education is effective in bringing about changes in people's knowledge and improving their oral health. However, the authors also state that it is unclear whether 'one-off' initiatives are sufficient to give significant oral health improvements for long periods. Like Schou and Locker, this Welsh review also suggests that there is evidence that programmes tailored to individuals have a greater chance of success and lead to longer-term change and that caries is best prevented by water fluoridation.

No one setting or target group emerged as being particularly appropriate for oral health promotion efforts. However, importantly the review echoes one of the findings of the current work in that whole-population health education initiatives may widen inequalities in oral health.

In general, two major differences between the current review and the Welsh review are notable. Firstly, the current review concludes that there is no overwhelming evidence that very specific, individually tailored programmes benefit the participants any more than simple direct instruction. This is in contrast to both the Welsh review and Schou and Locker's work, both of which conclude that individualistic programmes have a greater chance of success and lead to longer-term alterations in behaviour. Whilst this view is attractive and is consistent with many theories of behaviour change, close examination of the relevant studies reveals conflicting findings and very little hard evidence that long-term behaviour can be influenced. Of course, a natural consequence of the idiosyncratic approaches taken in 'tailor-made' interventions is that comparison of studies and synthesis of findings is virtually impossible. Thus, while such programmes may indeed be of value, it is simply not possible to say that sufficient evidence exists to support the adoption of such an approach.

A second conclusion drawn in the Welsh review is that increased knowledge leads to changes in behaviour. The literature reviewed here does not support such a view. The generally accepted criteria for causality dictate that, to support a hypothesis that x (knowledge) leads to y (a behaviour), the relationship must be consistently shown, must be shown to occur in the correct temporal order (change x precedes change y), must be specific (change x leads only to change y) and must be plausible. The relationship between knowledge levels and behaviour only achieves the last criterion – plausibility. Furthermore, as stated many times in this review, the instruments available for measuring 'oral health knowledge' are inconsistent and unvalidated and behaviour is generally measured using reported behaviour as a proxy indicator. Reported behaviour more probably measures knowledge than actual lifestyle and thus, although a consistent relationship between the two is consistently reported, this review must conclude that the balance of evidence is that the case for a causal relationship between knowledge and behaviour is 'not proven'.

Brown in 1994 published a review of 57 studies.[184] This review showed that many studies suffered from research design problems. In common with the current review, Brown concluded that knowledge and plaque control can be influenced by oral health promotion interventions but that long-term improvement is rarely demonstrated. Other outcomes such as attitudes and clinical disease levels showed much smaller improvements. Brown not only divided but also ranked outcome measures in the following order of importance:

1. Change in oral health measures.
2. Objective measure of behaviour change.
3. Self-reported behaviour change.
4. Change in knowledge or attitudes.
5. Awareness of programme.

Brown's review concluded that knowledge, attitudes, oral hygiene and gingival bleeding can all be improved through oral health promotion but that attitudes and objective measures of disease were less reliably influenced by oral health-promoting interventions.

10. Grey literature

Reports of varying levels of detail were received from many parts of the UK. Whilst very few provided sufficient detail to allow inclusion in a meta-analysis, or even any estimation of the intervention effect, this work is reported in order to demonstrate the breadth and scope of current oral health promotion practice in the UK. Field workers wrote to report several more interventions. However, those giving only a title are not included in this review. A list of known evaluative work in oral health promotion follows.

Instigator	Intervention	Methodology	Outcome
St Helens & Knowsley NHS Trust	Youth Taster Service.	Healthy snacks given to youngsters at taster evenings.	Youth clubs report changes in eating habits.
	Sugar-free desserts.	Evaluation of children's enjoyment of sugar-free desserts.	Not available
Chester and Halton NHS Trust	Peer-led DHE programme.	Peer leaders delivering DHE messages to colleagues.	All participants' knowledge improved.
			Increased confidence in peer leaders.
	Role of childminder in DHE.	DHE programme for childminders.	Increased knowledge among target group.
	School-based fluoride tablet scheme.	F tablets distributed via schools.	Several problems with continued participation.
North Derbyshire Community Health Care Service	Information pack to new parents.	Information given, tooth-brushing encouraged, dental registration encouraged.	Not yet complete
	Toothbrushing club.	School-based brushing programme.	Long-term effectiveness in increasing knowledge and oral hygiene.
Homeless people and homeless families' oral health project	Resources, training and improved accessibility to care for homeless people.	Provision of toothbrush and toothpaste to homeless centres, training DHE sessions, introduction of referral pathway.	Programme 'well received'.

Instigator	Intervention	Methodology	Outcome
Guy's Hospital, UMDS, London	Dental health educator. Home visits to new parents + F tabs	DMF on entrance to school examined.	DMF.
University of Bristol	Raising carers' awareness of oral care.	Randomised controlled trials.	Not yet available
Mancunian Community Health NHS Trust	Dental health workshop for carers of people with profound disabilities.	Pre-/post-test of knowledge and behaviour.	Increase in knowledge and attitudes.
Northampton Health Care	Registration campaign	Involvement of practitioners plus public campaign.	Increase in registration ratio from 686 to 1338 (95%) in 3- to 5-year-olds.
Huddersfield NHS Trust	First Aid for Teeth workshop.	Information to school-teachers about prevention of and first aid for dental trauma.	Increased knowledge and intended behaviour.
	Smile Week	Discussions and tooth-brushing in school.	Increased knowledge
Bradford Community Health	OHP with mother at maternity hospital.	To encourage healthy oral care practices. Evaluated after 1 year by questionnaire	29% could not remember programme. No differences in behaviours in those with/without memory of of programme.
Bradford Community Health	OHE programme with schoolchildren (8- to 9-year-olds)	2 x 1 hr lessons in schools. MCQ questionnaire used to evaluate	Increase in knowledge
	Campaign re dental implications of drinks in feeding bottle.	Bottle + feeder-cup exchange	563 bottles traded in; 52% remembered campaign after 3 months.
	Identification and prevention for children with special needs.	Establishing multi-disciplinary links, providing therapy and advice.	Evaluation by registration rates (not yet complete)
	OHP re feeding and weaning of Pakistani Muslim infants.	Community link worker in discussion groups with mothers.	Questionnaire re behaviour (not yet complete)
Southampton Community Health Services NHS Trust	Provision of resources for teachers for use in National Curriculum.	Publication of oral health education pack for use at key stages 1 and 2.	Distribution and uptake. Acceptability, knowledge of children (not yet complete)
	Provision of dental pack at HV's eight-month visit.	Using HV to distribute information + toothbrush + paste to parents.	Only half parents remembered pack after 12 months.
Salford and Trafford Community NHS Trust	Use of school quiz to provide knowledge in junior schools with high levels of disease.	Pre-/post- OH score. Diet record of snacks. Quiz.	⋏ OH, consistent across schools, variable effect on snacking. High knowledge levels.

Instigator	Intervention	Methodology	Outcome
Coventry Health Authority	Publication of article re oral cancer.	Examination of numbers of patients presenting.	6 extra patients seen.
	Effect of Smile Week in encouraging patient registration.	Audit of calls to freephone number for accessing GDP services.	6 calls in fortnight prior to intervention 30 in 24 hours post-intervention.
Kidderminster Health Care Trust	Seminar for carers of special needs clients.	Questionnaire evaluation of seminars.	Increased knowledge among carers.

Several other activities in the field of oral health promotion are worthy of mention here, although no formal studies of their effect have been published.

For example, 'Chuck Sweets off the Check-out' is a national campaign aimed at having confectionery removed from food store and pharmacy check-outs. The campaign group holds action days and actively encourages community involvement by distributing starter packs and resources. The campaign has been remarkably successful. When the campaign began, only two supermarket chains had sweet-free check-outs, now 60% of all supermarket check-outs are sweet-free and sales of confectionery in supermarkets have fallen by 30%. Over the whole campaign, the predicted number of check-outs free of sweets has risen from 31% in 1992 to 67% in 1995. In practical terms, 20 million people, 4 million of them with children, can now shop for food without having to resist the temptation to buy confectionery.

A further association using health promotion tactics rather than a direct educative approach is the Toothfriendly organisation. This is an international association which operates by forming a partnership between dentistry and industry, with industry providing funds to enable dentists to promote non-cariogenic (sugar-free) confectionery carrying the Toothfriendly logo. The campaign has been successful with dentists and other dental personnel, with 64% recognising the logo and 67% supporting the use of such devices to discourage sucrose consumption.

However, despite professional support, consumer interest remains sparse – possibly because of the low availability of the products. Toothfriendly will continue to try to recruit companies to the scheme.

A further example of action which has succeeded in changing consumer behaviour is the Baby Drinks Campaign. This campaign is led by Action and Information on Sugars but involves nine voluntary health organisations. This pressure group has succeeded in reducing sales of sugared 'baby drinks' by 12% and their activities have encouraged four major baby drink manufacturers to introduce sugar-free products. The impact of these changes in consumption on child dental health has yet to be measured.

Appendices

Appendix A. Tables of studies

(N/S signifies 'not stated')

Table 3.1. Randomised controlled trials – caries

Study	Quality score	Target population	Setting	Intervention	Results given	Conclusion	Follow-up	Mean intervention effect
Horowitz et al.[9]	16	279 children Expt 111 Control 168	School	Twice daily plaque removal at school under supervision for 4 yrs	Plaque, gingival inflammation and caries	Limited effectiveness – changes in OH not permanent	Immediate (past 4 years)	DMFS −0.62
Axelson et al.[10]	16	222 children Expt 151 Control 76	School	2–3 monthly prophylaxis plus OHI with active involvement over 6 years	Plaque scores. Periodontal probing depth, caries	Plaque, periodontal disease, gingivitis and caries all improved by intervention	Immediate (past 6 years)	DMFS (approximal) −2.5
Craig, Suckling and Pearce[11]	12	138 children Expt 97 Control 41	Clinic	Fortnightly OHI and professional prophylaxis plus F rinse	Plaque scores, caries increment	No difference in caries increment due to expensive professional intervention. F rinsing effective	5 months	DFS −0.5
Blinkhorn and Wight[12]	13	178 children Expt 91 Control 87	Clinic	Chairside education re diet, OH, F tablets dispensed to 11- to 13-year-olds attending for dental care in socially deprived area	DMFT, cost of treatment needed, no. of referrals for periodontal treatment	No noticeable effect on caries increment or referral for periodontal treatment, or treatment costs	1 year	DMFT −0.13
Stiefel, Rolla and Truelove[13]	15	38 handicapped adults Expt 29 Control 9	Community	Fortnightly prophylaxis and F gel, individual OHI v. group OHI over 40 weeks to disabled adults	Plaque scores, calculus, gingivitis pocket depth, DMFS	No improvements in plaque levels. Professional prophylaxis more effective than F	N/S	DMFS −2.8
Holt et al.[14]	11	Not given	N/S	Three home visits by dental health educator to mothers of very young children. Advice, leaflets and F drops	Diet, flucride use, oral hygiene practice (questionnaire)	Greater use of F and lower use of sweetened comforters. Home visits effective even with low social class	N/S	N/S

Table 3.1. Randomised controlled trials – caries (continued)

Study score	Quality	Target population	Setting	Intervention	Results given	Conclusion	Follow-up	Mean intervention effect
Ekman and Persson[15]	9	281 parents Expt 150 Control 131	Community	Information to parents of 6- to 27-month children at child care centre	Parental knowledge, attitudes and behaviours. Prevalence of caries at 3 years old	Early information tailored to parents' needs (and in own language) gives substantial reduction in caries frequency	+ 24 months	DFS –2.7
		Total No. 1136 Total Expt 629 Total Control 512						Overall ↗ D(M)FS = 1.8 95% CI = 0.384–3.264

Table 3.2. Quasi-experimental studies – caries

Study	Quality score	Target population	Setting	Intervention	Results given	Conclusion	Follow-up	Mean intervention effect
Blount and Stokes[16]	16	Children (pre-school) Expt 6 Control 11	Community School	Home visits aimed at helping parents help children to brush. Plaque measured at school			3–12 months	Not available
Schein, Tsamtsouris and Rovero[17]	11	Expectant adults Expt 150 Control 150	Community (hospital)	Dental health education as part of prenatal counselling			24 months	Not available
Axelsson and Lindhe[18]	12	Adults Expt 375 Control 180	Clinic	Instruction and active participation in oral hygiene techniques	Caries increment dramatically reduced	Oral hygiene instruction is effective in controlling caries	6 years	DFS 13.6 reduction
Wight and Blinkhorn[19]	17	Children Expt 677 Control 390	School	Dental health education in school. Dental health education in mobile unit	Caries measured using DMFT. No significant differences	No change in caries between test and control group	2 months	DMFT 0.14
Fogels et al.[20]	15	Children Expt 109 Control 109	Community	Supervised brushing in classroom	Reduction in caries increment	Supervised brushing effective in controlling caries	1 year	DFS 1.95
Lalloo and Solanki[21]	13	Children Expt 110 Control 102	School	Supervised daily brushing plus annual dental care at school	Post-test data only. DMFS	Test and control groups: significantly different mean DMFS	3 years	DMFS 4.18
Kerebel et al.[22]	12	Children (N not given)	School	Daily supervised brushing plus regular fluoride treatment	Slight effect on caries in deciduous dentition. Significant effect on caries in permanent teeth	Daily brushing plus fluoride is effective during mixed dentition phase	N/S	defs 0.34 DMF 2.23
Rayner[23]	15	Children Expt 413 Control 145	School	Daily toothbrushing at school plus home visits and similar regime without home visits	No differences observed between test and control in dmft	Daily brushing etc. has no short-term effect on caries rates	2 months	dmft 0.1

Table 3.2. Quasi-experimental studies – caries (continued)

Study	Quality score	Target population	Setting	Intervention	Results given	Conclusion	Follow-up	Mean intervention effect
Blinkhorn, Taylor and Willcox[24]	15	Children Expt 677 Control 390	School	Oral hygiene instruction plus fluoride treatment v. school programme and daily fluoride tablet	No differences observed between either test group v. control	Neither regime affected caries rate	6 months	DMFT 1.3–0.11
Blinkhorn, Wight and Yardley[25]	13	497 children	School	Various educative efforts using parents, teachers, project work and therapists	No observable differences in caries rates	Dental health education in whatever form not effective in reducing caries	N/S	No difference with any intervention
Olsen, Brown and Wright[26]	12	Children Expt 172 Control 138	Community	Community health workers making home visits v. information in leaflet	No statistical differences in caries between test and control groups. Noticeable social class difference	Home visits seem to be slightly more effective	12 months	DMFT 0.29

Table 3.3. Pre-/post- single group interventions – caries

Study	Quality score	Target population	Setting	Intervention	Results given	Conclusion	Follow-up
Truin et al.[27]	9	N = 170 children (pre-school)	Clinics	Parents given educational material at birth of child + six weeks subsequently + regular check-up	DMFs apparently reduced	Effective intervention	Ongoing (9 years)
Mann et al.[28]	13	N = 39 handicapped adults	Clinic	Individual DHE including brushing instruction + scaling	DMFT increment 0.49 over study period	Inconclusive	Immediate
Peterson[29]	12	N = 112 adults	Workplace	Prophylaxis, DHE and regular fluoride treatments	DMFs increment 6.4 over study period	Inconclusive	1 year

Table 4.1. Randomised controlled trials – oral hygiene

Study	Quality score	Target population	Setting	Intervention	Results given	Conclusion	Follow-up	Mean intervention effect
Ambjörnsen and Rise[30]	18	138 elderly Expt 94 Control 44	Unknown	Individual instruction +/– demonstration of denture cleaning to well-elderly edentulous	% plaque on maxillary denture	Verbal instruction had short-term effect while demonstration gave long-term improvements in denture hygiene	6 months	% denture plaque 15.3%↓
Baab and Weinstein[31]	18	31 adults Expt 15 Control 16	Clinic	OHI using self-inspection index compared with traditional OHI	Plaque scores, gingival bleeding, oral hygiene skills	No difference in OH or gingival health after 6 months	N/S	Insufficient data
Holt et al.[32]	11	Not given	N/S	Three home visits by dental health educator to mothers of very young children. Advice, leaflets and F drops	Diet, fluoride use, oral hygiene practice (questionnaire)	Greater use of F and lower use of sweetened comforters. Home visits effective even with low social class	N/S	N/S
Horowitz[33]*	16	279 children Expt 111 Control 168	School	Twice daily plaque removal at school under supervision for 4 years	Plaque, gingival inflammation and and caries	Limited effectiveness, changes in OH not permanent	Immediate	Plaque index 0.8↓
Hetland, Midtun and Kristoffersen[34]*	18	71 adults	Workplace	Adults receiving OHI by para-professionals with or without removal of plaque retentive factors	Plaque scores, gingival index, periodontal pocketing, plaque retaining factors	Plaque, gingival inflammation and pocket depths reduced	2 weeks	Plaque index 0.61↓
Craig, Suckling and Pearce[11]	12	138 children Expt 97 Control 41	Clinic	Fortnightly OHI and professional prophylaxis plus F rinse	Plaque scores, caries increment	Improvement in plaque levels due to professional intervention	5 months	PHP score 2.5↓

* denotes studies included in overall intervention effect (meta-analysis)

Table 4.1. Randomised controlled trials – oral hygiene (continued)

Study	Quality score	Target population	Setting	Intervention	Results given	Conclusion	Follow-up	Mean intervention effect
Bickley, Shaw and Shaw[35]*	17	29 handicapped adults Expt 16 Control 13	Adult training centre	Clinical photographic records used to motivate OH in mentally handicapped patients	Plaque scores	All participants (intervention and control): OH improved during study but subsequently relapsed	Immediate	Plaque index 0.6 ↓
Tedesco et al.[36]	13	167 adults Expt 111 Control 56	Community clinic	Viewing of active mobile bacteria taken from participant's mouth, cognitive restructuring + OHI	Plaque index, gingival index, self-efficacy, reasoned action and reported behaviour	OHI alone as effective as OH + other components but relapse delayed in intervention groups	9 months	Plaque index 0.09 ↓
Alcouffe[37]	13	26 adult (patients)	Neutral	Interview with psychologist for 1 hour. Non-directive analysis and exploratory listening	Plaque index	Interview had significant lasting effect on plaque levels	+ 2 years	Plaque score 18.7% ↓
Dowey[38]	12	203 children Expt 147 Control 54	School	Computer games in primary schools for 9- to 10-year-olds	Knowledge levels, oral hygiene	Knowledge most improved using traditional teaching plus computer. Neither group improved OH	3 months	Insufficient data
Söderholm et al.[39]	16	69 adults	Clinic	Plaque control taught in 3 visits. 30-minute sessions compared with 15 minutes	Plaque scores	No differences between groups after 12 weeks/after 24 months. Comprehensive OHI no more beneficial than basic OHI	12 weeks 4 years	% plaque per tooth 38.4 ↓
Albandar et al.[40]	16	227 children Expt 151 Control 76	School	OHP programmes based on individual needs and involving parents	Plaque scores, gingival bleeding	Gingival status and OH improved with individual comprehensive programme. OHI gave no improvement	Immediate	Plaque index 5.45 ↓

Table 4.1. Randomised controlled trials – oral hygiene (continued)

Study	Quality score	Target population	Setting	Intervention	Results given	Conclusion	Follow-up	Mean intervention effect
Lee [41]	15	55 children Expt 29 Control 26	School	OHI with/without use of a chart with 2 groups	Plaque index, gingival index	Brushing behaviour improved by chart but no effect on plaque or gingivitis	3 months	Insufficient data
Stiefel, Rolla and Truelove [13]*	15	38 handicapped adults Expt 29 Control 9	Community	Fortnightly prophylaxis + F gel, individual OHI v. group OHI over 40 weeks to disabled adults	Plaque scores, calculus, gingivitis pocket depth, DMFS	No improvements in plaque levels. Professional prophylaxis more effective than F	N/S	Plaque index 0.08↓
Knazen [42]	15	39 elderly Expt 23 Control 16	Clinic	OHP using PRECEDE framework. 4 appointments at 2-week intervals. 6-month follow-up	Debris index, gingival index, oral health index, denture plaque index	Time-consuming but effective programme. Most clinical parameters improved	6 months	Denture Plaque index 0.81↓
Bullen et al. [43]	14	50 pre-school children Expt 24 Control 26	Clinic	Toothbrushing instruction for parents of pre-school children. Participation v. observation. 4-week follow-up	Gingival index, plaque index	Plaque reduced in participatory group. No differences in gingival health	4 weeks	Modified plaque index 0.32↓
Bowen [44]	14	65 young adults Expt 29 Control 27	Clinic	Series of OHI visits with/without use of phase contrast microscopy	Plaque scores	Improvement in both groups but no additional effect with phase contrast microscopy	3 months	Plaque index↓
McCaul, Glasgow and O'Neill [45]	13	45 young adults	N/S	Three groups of adults taught skills and self-monitoring with additional components	Reported behaviours	Behavioural changes similar regardless of type of intervention. Excellent adherence during study but no long-term changes	2–6 months	PHP index 4%

* denotes studies included in overall intervention effect (meta-analysis)

Table 4.1. Randomised controlled trials – oral hygiene (continued)

Study	Quality score	Target population	Setting	Intervention	Results given	Conclusion	Follow-up	Mean intervention effect
Stewart et al.[46]*	14	100 adults	Clinic	Cognitive-behavioural, educative and attention control OHP programme with 21–65 male adults	Plaque index, self-report brushing and flossing behaviour	Plaque levels decreased in all groups, significantly more in cognitive-behavioural intervention group. Flossing increased in all groups	2 weeks	Plaque index 0.25▼
Boyd[47]	14	24 children Expt 16 Control 8	Orthodontic clinic	Use of Plak-lite for OHI in 9- to 14-year-old orthodontic patients	Plaque index, gingival index	Use of self-observation of plaque reinforces good oral hygiene	5 months	Plaque index per tooth 1.17▼
Glavind, Zeuner and Attström[48]	14	24 adults	Dental school	OHI using self-instruction in adult patients attending dental school	Plaque scores and gingival bleeding	No improvement in OH	5 weeks	% plaque score 2.0▼
Yeung, Howell and Fahey[49]*	14	62 adolescents Expt 33 Control 29	Orthodontic clinic	Weekly OHI and review with adolescent orthodontic patients	Bleeding index, plaque index, crevicular fluid volume, pocket probing depths	Improvement except in probing depths. Repetition brings about lasting behaviour change	4+ years	Plaque index 1.94▼
Price and Kiyak[50]	14	108 adults	Dental practice (N/S)	Behaviour modification plus education with non-institutionalised elderly. Follow-up 2–3 weeks	Objective and perceived oral health, self-reported behaviours and beliefs	Behaviour modification technique led to improved OH behaviours and beliefs	6–12 months	% plaque 0.1▼
		Total 2217 Expt 1038 Control 1179	Mean intervention effect (plaque index studies)					0.316 95% CI (–0.063, 0.695)

* denotes studies included in overall intervention effect (meta-analysis)

Table 4.2. Quasi-experimental studies – plaque control

Study	Quality score	Target population	Setting	Intervention	Results given	Conclusion	Follow-up	Mean intervention effect
Klass and Rhoden[51]	16	Children (pre-school) Expt 6 Control 11	School	Home visits and DHE re plaque control	N/S	N/S	3–12 months	N/S
Croft[52]	13	N/S adults	Clinic	Information re plaque control + reduction in fees if plaque control good	Improvement in both experimental groups but much greater in fee reduction group	Monetary incentive for plaque control is effective	6 months	18% difference between test + control
Croucher et al[53]	9	Children (pre-school) Expt 66 Control 23	Community	School + home reinforcement for OHI v. school reinforcement only v. Good Teeth Programme only	Increased numbers of children with clean teeth	Home + school reinforcement most effective in encouraging plaque control	6 months	6% more children with zero plaque score
Davis and Costanzo[54]	14	91 children	School	Flossing instruction via film, teacher and DSA	Children who had personal instruction showed slight improvement	Ineffective intervention	2 months	Plaque score 30% difference between test + control
Murray and and Epstein[55]	14	Children Expt 5 Control 5	School	Videotape presentation of toothbrushing technique	Plaque control measured using PHP index	Numbers too small to draw conclusions	Immediate	N/S
Kiyak and Mulligan[56]	13	Elderly Expt 24 Control 12	Community	Self-monitoring of OH practices +/- group discussions	No data reported	No data reported	6 months 6 weeks	Data not reported
Schwarz[57]	12	Adults Expt 3 733 Control 15 745	Community	Government paid for 75% cost of dental visits	No numerical data reported	No numerical data reported	Immediate	Data insufficient
Craft, Croucher and Dickinson[58]	11	Children Expt 835 Control 399	School	Education re plaque, caries, oral hygiene	Improvements in plaque control	Improvements variable	6 months	Complex data
Ivanovic and Lekic[59]	16	Children Expt 160 Control 80	Clinic School	DHE, toothbrushing instruction +/- flossing	Insufficient data	Insufficient data	6 months	N/S

Table 4.2. Quasi-experimental studies – plaque control (continued)

Study	Quality score	Target population		Setting	Intervention	Results given	Conclusion	Follow-up	Mean intervention effect
Melsen and Agerbaek[60]	12	Children Expt Control	81 83	School	Self-monitoring of OH practices +/– group discussions	Plaque control slightly improved	Intervention effective in encouraging plaque control	1 year	Plaque index reduced by 0.8
Ehudin and Martin[61]	10	Children Expt Control	175 100	School	Education to older children who subsequently taught younger ones	No effect on plaque levels	Intervention ineffective	1 week	No significant effect
McGlynn et al.[62]	14	Adults Expt	59	Clinic	Self-instruction manual + charting of OH behaviour + self-reward system	All patients benefited. Self-charting appeared to add benefit	Intervention effective but method immaterial	3 months	30%–50% plaque reduction
Glavind, Zeuner and Attström[63]	14	Adults Expt	37	Clinic	Self-instruction manual +/– instruction from hygienist	Similar improvements in all groups	Intervention effective but method immaterial	3 months	40% plaque reduction
Glavind et al.[64]	17	Adults Expt Control	47 27	Clinic	Self-examination +/– oral hygiene instruction	Plaque reduced in both experimental and control groups	Self-examination gave no added benefit	6 months	35% plaque reduction
Scruggs, Warren and Levine[65]	15	Children (diabetic) Expt Control	11 14	Clinic	Education plus rewards for good oral hygiene	No major differences	Intervention not effective	Immediate	No significant change
Schou et al.[66]	14	Elderly Expt Control	87 32	Community	Education re denture hygiene to individuals or to carers or both	Difficult to interpret	Some individuals benefited	2 months	N/S

Table 4.2. Quasi-experimental studies – plaque control (continued)

Study	Quality score	Target population		Setting	Intervention	Results given	Conclusion	Follow-up	Mean intervention effect
McGuire et al.[67]	13	Adults Expt Control	74 25	Clinic	DHE in 4 sessions + flossing. 1 month instruction recall	No significant difference in PHP score	Intervention ineffective	2–24 months	0.89 in PHP score
Shaw and Shaw[68]	15	Handicapped adults Expt Control	247 82	Community	Daily supervision of toothbrushing with different periods between reinforcement	No significant differences	Intervention ineffective	N/S	0.4 change in plaque score
Craft et al.[69]	11	Children Expt Control	216 194	School	Specifically designed educational programme + diary to record oral hygiene	No significant differences	Intervention ineffective	6 months	No significant difference
Soderhölm and Egelberg[70]	14	Adults Expt Control	39 20	Clinic	Plaque control instruction + use of disclosure wafers in sessions of varying frequency	25% reduction in plaque scores in experimental group. No change in control	Both programmes effective for plaque reduction	12 weeks	25% reduction in plaque
Kerebel et al.[22]	12	Children Expt	244	School	Education to children and parents plus supervised daily brushing + fluoride treatment	No improvement in control, plaque reduced in experimental group	Effective intervention	Immediate	305 reduction in plaque
Emier et al.[72]	14	Children Expt Control	36 25	School	Lecture about dental health plus tooth-brushing lesson or 4 home visits	Home visit group showed greatest improvements in plaque control	Home visits more effective than single lesson (girls more than boys)	44 weeks	30%–40% reduction in plaque
Julien[73]	17	Children Expt Control	163 153	School	Workshop for parents and teachers. OHI and awards for children	Plaque scores worsened in both test and control group	Ineffective intervention	1 year	Non-significant results
Rayner[23]	15	Children (pre-school)		School	Supervised daily brushing +/– home visits	Plaque scores most improved in group with home visits with or without brushing	Home visits effective	2 months	50% reduction in plaque

Table 4.2. Quasi-experimental studies – plaque control (continued)

Study	Quality score	Target population		Setting	Intervention	Results given	Conclusion	Follow-up	Mean intervention effect
Houle[75]	12	Children Expt Control	81 51	School	School-based programme + visit from hygienist v. hygienist alone	No difference between control + hygienist group. Those with school programme had marginally cleaner teeth	Intervention not effective for improving OH	4 months	No significant differences
Cutress et al.[76]	12	Adults Expt Control	548 321	Community	Provision of tooth-brushing + education + scaling	No observable differences between groups	Insufficient data	Immediate	Complex data
Tan, Ruiter and Verhey[77]	9	Adults Expt Control	77 127	Workplace	Dental health care + instruction + prophylaxis	Plaque control improved in experimental group	Intervention effective	6 months	23% plaque reduction
Schou[78]	15	Adults Expt Control	68 68	Workplace	Peer group DHE session repeated five times	Plaque control improved in experimental group	Intervention effective	3½ years	60% plaque reduction
Hodge et al.[79]	14	Children Expt Control	193 167	School	Teeth for Life programme plus toothbrushing at 4 weekly sessions	No observable differences between groups	Ineffective intervention	1 week	No significant differences
Craft, Croucher and Blinkhorn[80]	10	Children Expt Control	1092 399	School	Natural Nashers school programme	No consistent differences between experimental and control	Ineffective intervention	6 months	Complex data
Arnold and Doyle[81]	13	Children Expt Control	114 66	School	Natural Nashers school programme	No difference between test and control in plaque scores	Ineffective intervention	6 months	Complex data
Goodkind et al.[82]	13	Children Expt Control	411 93	School	Children given DHE from parents, teachers through project or from hygienist	No major differences between groups	Ineffective intervention	Immediate	Complex data

Table 4.2. Quasi-experimental studies – plaque control (continued)

Study	Quality score	Target population		Setting	Intervention	Results given	Conclusion	Follow-up	Mean intervention effect
Olser, Brown and Wright[26]	12	Children Expt Control	172 138	Community	DHE via home visits compared with same information via pamphlet	No observable differences	Ineffective intervention	12 months	No significant difference
Wight[84]	9	Children Expt Control	303 297	School	Chairside DHE plus school-based DHE programme	No observable differences	Inconclusive	N/S	Complex data
Sutcliffe, Rayner and and Brown[85]	13	Children (pre-school) Expt Control	272 247	School	Professional instruction on toothbrushing plus daily supervised brushing	Improved OH in experimental group	Effective intervention	1 year	30% improvement in debris index

Table 4.3. Pre-/post- single group interventions – plaque

Study	Quality score	Target population	Setting	Intervention	Results given	Conclusion	Follow-up	Mean intervention effect
Hölund[86]	14	N = 344 children	School	Monthly brushing instruction. Reward for OH for 120 participants	Plaque levels reduced by approximately 20%	Improvement in plaque control	1 month	20% ↓
Croft[52]	10	N = 780 children	School	Daily disclosure and brushing. Flossing for older children	Plaque levels in younger children reduced by approximately 40%	Improvement in plaque control	Immediate. Ongoing	40% ↓
Scanlan[88]	11	N = 76 children (pre-school)	School	Good Teeth programme	Reductions in plaque. Increase in No. of plaque-free children	Improvement in plaque control	15 weeks	N/A
Lundstrom and Hamp[89]	11	N = 60 children	Clinic	OHI, fortnightly prophylaxis, fortnightly fluoride rinses	No numerical data	Insufficient data	30 months	N/A
Bergstrom[90]	14	N = 50 adults	Workplace	Attendance at dental faculty course	No observable differences	Intervention not effective	Immediate	
Bader et al.[91]	12	N = 78 adults	Clinic	Instruction on use of electric toothbrush + take-home manual	40–50% reductions in plaque levels	Effective intervention	Immediate	40% ↓
Odman, Lange and Bakdash[92]	10	N = 22 adults	Clinic	OHI and skills training + self-instruction manual	34% reduction in plaque scores	Effective intervention	Immediate	30% ↓
Messer[93]	12	N = 6 children	School	Learning by teaching younger children	35% reduction in oral hygiene index	Effective intervention	N/S	35% ↓
Heasman, Jacobs and Chapple[94]	14	N = 93 adults	Clinic	Scaling, root planing, prophylaxis, OHI by hygienist	Approximately 35% reduction in plaque	Effective intervention	6 months	N/A
Brown, Morilleau and Cross[95]	11	N = 52 children	School	Toothbrushing instruction + supervision	Approximately 40% reduction in plaque	Effective intervention	Immediate	N/A

Table 4.3. Pre-/post- single group interventions – plaque (continued)

Study	Quality score	Target population	Setting	Intervention	Results given	Conclusion	Follow-up
Jodaiken[96]	11	N = 114 children	School	DHE by teachers who were instructed by dentist	Small reduction in plaque levels	Inconclusive	6 months
Towner[97]	9	N = 59 children	School	Gleam Team programme delivered	Attitudes and beliefs profoundly affected	Inconclusive	4 weeks
Simmons, Smith and Gelbier[98]	10	N = 420 children (pre-school)	School	Children taught how to brush by therapist	Data difficult to interpret	Brushing skills improved slightly	9 weeks
Schou, Wight and Wohlgemuth[99]	11	N = 874 children	School	One lesson on dental health matters	Increase in choosing safe snacks. Reported brushing behaviour improved	Partly effective	1 week
Rich, Friedman and Schultz[100]	10	N = 53 children	Clinic	Information about brushing and general oral health. Rewards for good humour	No numerical data	Inconclusive	Immediate
Weinstein et al.[101]	9	N = 5 adults	School	Brushing instruction using models + general DHE	Increased time spent brushing. More thorough brushing	Inconclusive due to small number of participants	2 weeks
Petersen and Nörtov[102]	8	N = 235 elderly	Clinic	Free dental health service + prophylaxis + scaling + OHI + advice	Placed greater value on teeth + oral hygiene increased	Effective intervention	Immediate
Honkala et al.[103]	9	N = 4025 children	Clinic	Annual treatment and DHE session provided	Data incompletely reported	Inconclusive	Ongoing
Benitez, O'Sullivan and Tinanoff[104]	11	N = 17 children (pre-school)	Clinics	Parents instructed re brushing children's teeth + apply F gel	Data incompletely reported	Inconclusive	Immediate

Table 4.3. Pre-/post- single group interventions – plaque (continued)

Study	Quality score	Target population	Setting	Intervention	Results given	Conclusion	Follow-up
Smorang and Erikson[105]	9	$N = 170$ adults (handicapped)	Workplace	Nursing staff taught how to give oral care to their charges	No numerical data	Inconclusive	3 months
Thomas[106]	6	$N = N/S$ adults	N/S	Public health nurses given training about oral care	No quantitative data	Inconclusive	1 week
Weisenberg, Kegeles and Lund[107]	12	$N = 214$ children	School	Slide show demonstration + active participation + fluoride treatments	No changes	Intervention not effective	Immediate

Table 5.1. Randomised controlled trials – gingival health

Study	Quality score	Target population	Setting	Intervention	Results given	Conclusion	Follow-up
Yeung, Howell and Fahey[49]	14	62 children Expt 33 Control 29	Clinic	Weekly OHI review and review in clinic	Bleeding, crevicular fluid volume improved. Pocket probing depths not improved	Effective intervention	4 years
Horowitz et al.[9]	16	279 Expt 111 Control 168	School	Twice daily plaque removal at school under supervision for 4 years	Plaque, gingival inflammation improved but not permanently	Limited effectiveness	Immediate
Knazan[42]	15	39 elderly Expt 23 Control 16	Clinic	Oral health education using PRECEDE framework. 4 appts at 2-week intervals	Debris, gingivitis and denture plaque improved	Effective but time-consuming	6 months
Baab and Weinstein[115]	18	31 adults Expt 15 Control 16	Clinic	OHI +/– self-inspection index compared with traditional OHI	No differences in oral hygiene or gingival health	Intervention not effective	6 months
Lee[41]	15	55 children Expt 29 Control 26	School	Oral hygiene instruction +/– use of chart	Reported brushing behaviour improved but no change in plaque or gingivitis	Intervention not effective	3 months
Boyd[47]	14	24 children Expt 16 Control 8	Clinic	Use of Plak-lite during OHI	Plaque and gingival indices improved	Effective intervention	5 months
Tedesco, Keffer and Davis[116]	13	167 adults Expt 11 Control 156	Clinic	Viewing of active mobile bacteria taken from participant's mouth + OHI + cognitive restructuring	Plaque and gingival health improved then relapsed. Less relapse in cognitive group	Limited effectiveness	9 months

Table 5.1. Randomised controlled trials – gingival health (continued)

Study	Quality score	Target population	Setting	Intervention	Results given	Conclusion	Follow-up
Stiefel, Rolla and Truelove[13]	15	38 handicapped adults Expt 29 Control 9	Clinic	Fortnightly prophylaxis + F gel + OHI individually or in groups	No improvements in plaque. Professional prophylaxis more effective than FΘ	Intervention not effective	40 weeks
Hetland, Midtun and Kristoffersen[34]	18	71 adults	Workplace	Adults receiving OHI from professional staff with or without removal of plaque retentive factors	Plaque, gingival inflammation and pocket depths reduced	Effective intervention	2 weeks
Bullen et al.[43]	14	Children (pre-school) Expt 24 Control 26	Clinic	Toothbrushing instruction for parents of pre-school children. Participation v. observation	Plaque reduced but no difference in gingival health	Intervention not effective	4 weeks
Albandar et al.[117]	16	227 children Expt 151 Control 76	School	Oral health instruction based on individual needs and parental involvement	Gingival status and OH improved with comprehensive programme. OHI alone no improvement	Effective intervention	Immediate

Table 5.2. Quasi-experimental studies – gingival health

Study	Quality score	Target population		Setting	Intervention	Results given	Conclusion	Follow-up	Mean intervention effect
Feaver and Galgut[18]	13	Adults Expt	20	Workplace	Lecture, toothbrushing instruction, floss and disclosing tablets	Both interventions caused reduction in plaque and gingivitis	Effective intervention	3 months	36% plaque reduction 10% gingivitis reduction
Craft et al.[69]	11	Children Expt Control	835 399	School	Education re plaque, caries and oral hygiene by teachers	Both plaque and gingivitis improved by intervention	Oral hygiene improved by intervention	6 months	Complex data
Ivanovic and Lekic[59]	16	Children Expt Control	160 80	Clinic within school	Education at chairside	N/S	Some improvement. Type of intervention not important	6 months	Insufficient data
Melsen and Agerbaek[60]	12	Children Expt Control	81 83	School	Completion of oral hygiene charts. +/– group discussions	Plaque scores and gingivitis unaffected	No significant improvements	1 year	Plaque 0.08 Gingivitis 0.06
McGlynn et al.[62]	14	Adults and children Expt	59	Clinic	Self-instruction manual – fluoride use + charting of oral hygiene + self-rewards	All patients benefited, particularly new patients. Self-charting appeared to add benefit	Intervention effective. Self-monitoring of behaviour encourages oral hygiene practices	3 months	30–50% plaque reduction. 25–40% reduction in gingivitis
Glavind, Zeuner and Attström[63]	14	37 adults		Clinic	Self-instruction manual ± instruction by hygienist ± leaflet	Similar improvements in all groups	Intervention effective but method immaterial	3 months	40% plaque reduction. 25% bleeding reduction
Axelsson and Lindhe[18]	12	Adults Expt Control	375 180	Clinic	Prophylaxis + case presentation v. practice in oral hygiene technique	Nos. of deep pockets dramatically reduced in experimental groups	Effective intervention	Follow-up over 6 years	Reduction by 12% in nos of deep pockets
Glavind, Zeuner and Attström[119]	14	Adults Expt Control	47 27	Clinic	Self-examination +/– oral hygiene instruction	Plaque reduced in both experimental and control. Similar result for bleeding	Self-examination did not give added benefit	6 months	30–40% reduction in plaque and bleeding
Wight and Blinkhorn[19]	17	Children Expt Control	677 390	School	Education via clinic or teacher. F in tablets or gel	No major differences	Intervention not effective	2 months	0.14 reduction in gingivitis

Table 5.2. Quasi-experimental studies – gingival health (continued)

Study	Quality score	Target population	Setting	Intervention	Results given	Conclusion	Follow-up	Mean intervention effect
Scruggs, Warren and Levine[65]	15	Children (diabetic) Expt 11 Control 14	Clinic	Education plus rewards for good oral hygiene	No major differences	Intervention not effective	Immediate	0.1 difference in plaque index
Shaw and Shaw[68]	15	Handicapped Expt 247 Control 82	Community	Supervised brushing plus various oral hygiene reinforcement programmes	No major differences	Intervention not effective	N/S	Complex data
Craft et al.[69]	11	Children Expt 216 Control 194	School	Teachers using specifically designed school programme of DHE	No difference between test and control group in either plaque or gingivitis	Programme effective in changing knowledge but not oral hygiene	6 months	No significant difference
Söderholm and Egelberg[70]	14	Adults Expt 39 Control 20	Clinic	Dental health education given in course of 1 or 3 sessions	25% reduction in plaque scores in experimental groups. No change in control	Both oral health education programmes effective for plaque reduction	12 weeks	20–25% difference in plaque scores
Julien[73]	17	Children Expt 163 Control 153	School	Workshop for parents + OHI for children and reward system	No changes in plaque or gingivitis	Intervention not effective	1 year	No significant differences
Rayner[23]	15	Children (pre-school) Expt 413 Control 145	School	Supervised daily brushing +/– home visits	Home visits had more effect than daily brushing	Home visits improved plaque control but not gingivitis	2 months	50% plaque reduction
Cutress et al.[120]	12	Adults Expt 548 Control 321	Community	Various interventions aimed at improving oral hygiene	No observable differences	Insufficient data	Immediate	CPITN mean score reduction of 2.1
Tan, Ruiter and Verhey[77]	9	Adults Expt 77 Control 127	Workplace	Dental health care + instruction + prophylaxis	Calculus, pocketing and plaque levels improved in experimental group	Intervention effective	6 months	Plaque reduction 0.42

Table 5.2. Quasi-experimental studies – gingival health (continued)

Study	Quality score	Target population	Setting	Intervention	Results given	Conclusion	Follow-up	Mean intervention effect
Blinkhorn and Wight[12]	15	Children Expt 677 Control 390	School	Dental health education by hygienist or teachers. Fluoride in tablets or gel	No difference between the two interventions. Slightly higher prevalence of widespread gingivitis	Minimal improvements	Immediate	Gingivitis in more than 5 sites reduced by approximately 8%
Craft, Croucher and Dickinson[58]	10	Children Expt 1092 Control 399	School	Dental health education by teachers using specifically designed programme	Plaque levels improved in some schools. Gingivitis largely unaffected as only slightly improved	Programme ineffective in improving oral hygiene	6 months	Complex data
Blinkhorn, Wight and Yardley[25]	13	Children Expt 404 Control 93	School	DHE via teachers, parents, projects or therapist	No major differences between groups	No differences between different interventions	Immediate	Complex data
Lee[41]	15	Children (pre-school) Expt 57 Control 57	School	Supervised daily toothbrushing	Debris index lower in experimental group and oral health improved	Effective intervention	Immediate	OH Index Score reduction 19 in test 7 in control. Debris improved by 30%
Kallio and Ainamo[121]	14	Children Expt 785 Control 382	School	Teacher-led DHE programme +/– leaflet	Proportion of non-bleeding papillae improved in all groups	No differences between test and control	3 weeks	4–5% improvement in all groups
Zimmerman, Bornstein and Martinsson[122]	15	Children Expt 193	Clinic	Slide show plus individual OHI ± group discussion and follow-up OHI	Gingival bleeding reduced in test and control. Reduction in pocketing in test group	Gingivitis improved after 1 OHI session	3 months	30% reduction in gingival bleeding following 1 or more OHI

Table 5.3. Pre-/post- single group interventions – gingival health

Study	Quality score	Target population	Setting	Intervention	Results given	Conclusion	Follow-up	Mean intervention effect
Schou and Wight[123]	12	N = 342 children	School	20-minute sessions re oral hygiene + free toothbrush	No change in gingival bleeding score but lower proportion of high social class had no bleeding	Partly effective but only for less deprived children	4 months	
Takahashi et al.[124]	13	N = 33 adults	N/S	OHI given to periodontal patients by hygienist	Dramatic improvement in prevalence and depth of pockets	Effective intervention	40 daily	
Mann et al.[28]	13	N = 39 handicapped children	Clinic	Education plus professional scaling	Minor changes in numbers with poor periodontal status	Inconclusive	Immediate	
Lundstrom and Hamp[89]	11	N = 60 children	Clinic	OHI, fortnightly prophylaxis, fortnightly fluoride rinse	Insufficient data	Inconclusive	30 months	
Glassman et al.[125]	14	N = 66 handicapped children	School	Teacher undertook daily brushing	Approximately 25–30% reduction in debris score	Effective intervention	Immediate	25% ↓
Nikias, Budner and Breakstone[126]	10	N = 109 adults	Clinic Workplace	Visits to home or workplace by hygienist. Prophylaxis + OHI	All participants had high plaque levels at start. Effective for some participants	Inconclusive	24 weeks	N/A
Tenenbaum[127]	14	N = 50 adults	Workplace	Attendance at dental faculty course	No effect on gingival index	Intervention not effective	Immediate	
Bergstrom[90]	12	N = 78 adults	Clinic	Instruction on use of electric toothbrush + take home manual	Reduction in number of sites with bleeding	Partly effective intervention	Immediate	

Table 6.1. Randomised controlled trials – knowledge

Study	Quality score	Target population	Setting	Intervention	Results given	Conclusion	Follow-up
McCaul, Glasgow and O'Neill[45]	13	45 adults	N/S	Three groups of adults taught skills and self-monitoring +/- additional components	Reported behaviour change for all types of intervention	Short-term change. Long-term relapse	6 months
Dowey[38]	12	Children Expt 149 Control 54	School	Computer games in primary school for teaching DHE to 9- to 10-year-olds	Knowledge improved especially when traditional teaching + computer usage	Knowledge changed. Behaviour did not	3 months
Hartshorne et al.[128]	11	134 children Expt 89 Control 145	School	Educational intervention plus support for parents	No data provided	Inconclusive	2 months
Moltzer and Hoogstraten[129]	12	92 adults	Clinic	3 months of oral health instruction using film, film plus discussion or standard programme	Knowledge, attitudes, diet, brushing behaviour all changed (measured by questionnaires)	DHE effective. Method is immaterial	6 months
Hoogstraten and Moltzer[130]	10	108 adults	Clinic	30 min. instruction on OH by hygienist +/- educational film	Knowledge, attitude, fear all changed	Personal instruction effective even after 6 months	12 months
Ekman and Persson[15]	9	281 adults Expt 150 Control 131	Community	Information to parents of 6- to 27-month-old children at child care centre	Parental knowledge and attitudes changed	Information to parents reduces caries in children	24 months
Rantanen, Siirilä and Lehvilä[131]	14	89 adults	Clinic	Leaflet +/- personal instruction to prosthetic patients	Knowledge improved but behaviour did not	Effective intervention	12 months

Table 6.2. Randomised controlled trials – attitudes, behaviour, beliefs

Study	Quality score	Target population	Setting	Intervention	Results given	Conclusion	Follow-up
Tedesco, Keffer and Davis[116]	13	167 adults Expt 111 Control 56	Clinic	Viewing of active mobile bacteria taken from participant's mouth + cognitive restructuring + OHI	Reported toothbrushing behaviour + reasoned action behaviour increased	Changes in behaviour but relapse	9 months
Price and Kiyak[50]	14	108 elderly	Clinic	Behaviour modification plus education with non-institutionalised elderly	Improved OH behaviour and modified beliefs	Intervention effective	12 months
Hoogstraten and Moltzer[130]	10	108 adults – elderly Expt 23 Control 16	Clinic	30 minutes OH instruction by hygienist	Knowledge, attitudes and behaviour change. Film no effect	Intervention effective	12 months
Moltzer and Hoogstraten[129]	12	92 adults	Clinic	3 months of oral health instruction using film, film plus discussion or standard programme	Knowledge, attitudes and beliefs changed	Intervention effective	6 months
Malvitz and Broderick[132]	13	40 adults	Clinic	Adults given information by hygienist	Knowledge, attitudes and reported behaviour altered	Intervention effective	6 months
Alcouff[133]	13	40 adults	N/S	At-risk adults given social-cognitive intervention or skills training or self-monitoring	Reported behaviours but relapsed	Intervention effective. Method of no consequence	6 months
Ekman and Persson[15]	9	281 adults Expt 150 Control 131	Community	Information to parents of 6- to 27-month-old children at child care centre	Parental knowledge, attitude + behaviour all changed	Effective intervention	24 months

Table 6.2. Randomised controlled trials – attitudes, behaviour, beliefs (continued)

Study	Quality score	Target population	Setting	Intervention	Results given	Conclusion	Follow-up	Mean intervention effect
McCaul, Glasgow and O'Neill[45]	13	40 young adults	N/S	Adults at risk for 'gum disease' given social-cognitive or skills training or self-monitoring	Reported behaviours	All programmes improved OH behaviour during study but all relapsed	2 months	PHP index 4%
Dulac, Ivory and Horowitz[134]	11	134 children Expt 89 Control 45	Schools	Educational intervention plus support for parents	No data provided	Paper argues for support for parents in conjunction with school-based activity	2 months	Insufficient data
Glavind, Zeuner and Attström[119]	10	55 adults Expt 29 Control 26	Clinic	OHI using self-educational programmes compared with personal instruction by dentist	% plaque score (grouped data only)	Self-instruction and advice from GDP equally successful in teaching OHI. Improvements maintained for 6 months	Effective intervention	Insufficient data

Table 6.3. Quasi-experimental studies – knowledge

Study	Quality score	Target population	Setting	Intervention	Results given	Conclusion	Follow-up
Uitenbroek et al.[135]	14	Adults Expt 159 Control 302	Clinic	Patients attending practice with or without hygienist advice	Knowledge improved marginally	Hygienists have small effect on knowledge levels	N/S
Craft et al.[69]	11	Children Expt 835 Control 399	School	DHE provided by teachers	Substantial improvement in knowledge levels	Effective intervention	6 months
Peterson and Rubinson[136]	12	Children Expt 230 Control 230	School	Dental health lessons at school	Insufficient data	Inconclusive	6 weeks
Craft, Croucher and Blinkhorn[80]	11	Children Expt 216 Control	School	Natural Nashers school programme	Substantial improvements in knowledge	Effective intervention	6 months
ter Horst and Hoogstraten[137]	13	Children Expt 253 Control 172	School	Film re plaque and periodontal disease	Increased knowledge after intervention	Effective intervention	2 months
Lachapelle, Desaulniers and Bujold[138]	15	Children Expt 511 Control 155	School	Sound + slide presentation on caries and oral hygiene	No significant improvement in knowledge	Intervention ineffective	6 months
Tan Ruiter and Verhey[77]	9	Adults Expt 43 Control 42	Workplace	DHE + professional prophylaxis + group discussions	Substantial improvement in knowledge	Effective intervention	6 months
Schou[78]	15	Adults Expt 68 Control 68	Workplace	DHE to peer groups repeated at 5 monthly intervals	Substantial improvements in knowledge	Effective intervention	3½ years
Laiho et al.[139]	11	Children Expt 312 Control 146	School	Lecture and slide show on general DHE	Programme improved male students' knowledge. Little effect on females	Some effect from intervention	2 months

Table 6.3. Quasi-experimental studies – knowledge (continued)

Study	Quality score	Target population		Setting	Intervention	Results given	Conclusion	Follow-up
Craft, Croucher and Dickinson[58]	10	Children Expt Control	677 390	School	4 x per year instruction from dental hygienist +/– Yours for Life instruction by teachers	Substantial improvements in knowledge	Effective intervention	Immediate
Arnold and Doyle[81]	13	Children Expt Control	1114 66	School	Natural Nashers taught by teachers	Some areas of knowledge improved	Partly effective intervention	6 months
Wright[84]	9	Children Expt Control	303 297	School	Chairside dental health education + school-based programme	Results variable	Inconclusive	N/S
Søgaard and Holst[140]	12	Children Expt Control	541 500	School	Dental health programme for 1 week in school	No significant differences between groups	Intervention	3 weeks
Walsh[141]	11	Children Expt Control	399 240	Hygienist instruction + supervised toothbrushing and flossing	Substantial increase in knowledge	Knowledge levels increased	Effective intervention	Immediate

Table 6.4. Quasi-experimental studies – attitudes + beliefs

Study	Quality score	Target population		Setting	Intervention	Results given	Conclusion	Follow-up	Mean intervention effect
Goepferd[142]	13	Adults (mothers) Expt Control	74 66	Community	DHE in clinic	Positive improvement in intentions and attitudes	Effective intervention	4 weeks	N/A
Uitenbroek et al.[135]	14	Adults Expt Control	159 302	Clinic	Hygienist counselling at practice	More positive attitudes and perceptions in test group	Effective intervention	N/S	N/A
Kiyak and Mulligan[56]	13	Elderly Expt Control	24 12	Community	Group discussion, self-monitoring of OHI and praise	Data not reported	Data not reported	N/S	N/A
Craft et al.[69]	11	Children Expt Control	835 399	School	Education in classroom by teacher	Reported attitudes dramatically more favourable in experimental group	Intervention improved attitudes	6 months	4–51% improvement
Craft, Croucher and Blinkhorn[80]	11	Children Expt Control	216 194	School	Natural Nashers school DHE programme	Improvement in attitude for all items	Intervention improves attitudes	6 months	N/A
ter Horst and Hoogstraten[137]	13	Children Expt Control	253 172	School	Film detailing plaque control and periodontal disease	No observable difference between test and control	Intervention not effective	2 months	N/A
Lachapelle, Desaulniers and Bujold[138]	15	Children Expt Control	511 155	School	Sound + slide presentation v. verbal presentation of same information	No observable differences between experimental group + control	Intervention not effective	6 months	No significant difference
Tan, Ruiter and Verhey[77]	9	Adults Expt Control	77 127	Workplace	DHE + OHI + professional prophylaxis + group discussions	No differences between groups	Intervention not effective	6 months	No significant difference
Schou[78]	15	Adults Expt Control	68 68	Workplace	DHE in peer groups in 5 monthly sessions	Variable improvement in attitude depending on item	Inconclusive	3½ years	Complex data

Table 6.4. Quasi-experimental studies – attitudes + beliefs (continued)

Study	Quality score	Target population		Setting	Intervention	Results given	Conclusion	Follow-up	Mean intervention effect
Laiho et al.[139]	11	Children Expt Control	312 146	School	Lecture + slides v. older students teaching same materials	Most positive attitude towards lecture + slides	Older students engender negative attitudes, particularly in males	2 months	N/A
Craft et al.[69]	10	Children Expt Control	1092 399	School	Natural Nashers programme	Improvement in attitude in almost all items	Programme effective in engendering positive attitudes	6 months	N/A
Arnold and Doyle[81]	13	Children Expt Control	114 66	School	Natural Nashers programme	Improvement in attitude in almost all items	Programme effective in engendering positive attitudes	6 months	N/A
Wright[84]	9	Children Expt Control	303 297	School	Chairside DHE plus school programme	Difficult to interpret	Inconclusive	N/S	N/A
Søgaard et al.[144]	12	Children Expt Control	541 500	School	Dental health programme ± booklet re periodontal disease	Difficult to interpret	Inconclusive	3 weeks	N/A
Hölund[143]	10	Children Expt Control	59 55	School	Comparison of four methods of education	No observable effects on attitudes	Programmes not effective	2 months	N/A
Kleinman[145]	14	Children (diabetics) Expt Control	11 14	Clinic	DHE and OHI plus rewards for good OHI	No observable effect on health locus of control	Programme not effective	Immediate	N/A

Table 6.5. Quasi-experimental studies – behaviour

Study	Quality score	Target population		Setting	Intervention	Results given	Conclusion	Follow-up
Uitenbroek et al.[135]	14	Adults Expt Control	159 302	Clinic	Patients attending practice with or without hygienist advice	Reported self-care marginally improved	Inconclusive	N/S
Schein, Tsamtsouris and Rovero[17]	11	Adults Expt Control	150 150	Clinic	Parents attending prenatal classes given dental health counselling	No numerical data available	Inconclusive	24 months
Barrie and Carstens[146]	16	Children Expt Control	347 113	School	DHE ± supervised brushing either once or twice	Debris index improved	Inconclusive	17 weeks
Russell, Horovitz and Frazier[147]	11	Children Expt Control	238 53	School	Education ± sealants and/or prophylaxis	Knowledge only reported	Inconclusive	16 months
ter Horst and Hoogstraten[137]	13	Children Expt Control	253 172	School	Film re plaque and periodontal disease	No significant improvement in attitude to oral hygiene control	Ineffective intervention	2 months
Tan, Ruiter and Verhey[77]	9	Adults Expt Control	43 142	Workplace	DHE + professional prophylaxis + group discussions	Significant effect on toothbrushing behaviour	Effective intervention with respect to OH	6 months
Schou[78]	15	Adults Expt Control	68 68	Workplace	DHE to peer groups repeated at 5 monthly intervals	Improved brushing behaviour	Effective intervention	3½ years
Goodkind et al.[82]	13	Adults Expt Control	48 44	Clinic	4 hours' intensive instruction on denture care	No observable differences	Inconclusive	6 months
Milén et al.[148]	10	Children Expt Control	732 296	Clinic	DHE during free dental examination	No discernible effect	Intervention not effective	N/S

Table 6.5. Quasi-experimental studies – behaviour (continued)

Study	Quality score	Target population		Setting	Intervention	Results given	Conclusion	Follow-up
McIntyre, Wight and Blinkhorn[149]	12	Children Expt Control	209 101	School	DHE programme in schools	Improvement in snack choices. Other behaviours minimally affected	Inconclusive	5 months
Søgaard and Holst[140]	12	Children Expt Control	541 500	School	Dental health programme for 1 week in school	Insufficient data	Inconclusive	3 weeks
Walsh, Heckman and Moreau-Diettinger[150]	11	Children Expt Control	399 240	School	Hygienist instruction + supervised toothbrushing and flossing	Data for OH behaviour not reported	Inconclusive	Immediate
Robinson and Tappe[151]	14	Children (pre-school) Expt Control	112 51	School	Pre-school oral health programme to parents and children	Knowledge improved	Effective intervention	Immediate

Table 6.6. Pre-/post- single group interventions – knowledge

Study	Quality score	Target population	Setting	Intervention	Results given	Conclusion	Follow-up
Towner[97]	9	N = 50 children	School	Gleam Team programme run by teacher	Data complex. Knowledge slightly improved	Effective intervention	4 weeks
Schou, Wight and Wohlgemut[99]	11	N = 874 children	School	One lesson on dental health matters	Knowledge improved but not in all	Effective intervention	1 week
Peterson and Nörtov[102]	8	N = 235 elderly	Clinic	Free dental health services + prophylaxis + scaling + O-H + advice	Proportion of pupils with 'high' knowledge improved	Intervention probably effective	Immediate
Smorang and Erikson[105]	9	N = 170 adults	Workplace	Nursing staff taught how to give oral care to their charges	No numerical data	Inconclusive	3 months
Thomas[106]	6	N = N/S	N/S	Public health nurses given training about dental care	No quantitative data presented	Inconclusive	1 week
Holm[152]	11	N = 314 adults	Community	Advice given to mothers re sugar – also given toothbrush + fluoride drops	No follow-up data given	Inconclusive	Immediate
Peterson and Rubinson[153]	14	N = 476 children	School	5 lessons on oral health including home assignments	Increased % subjects giving correct answer to all questions	Effective intervention	N/S
Hartshorne al.[128]	13	N = 71 children	School	Teachers and pupils given OHE/OHI	Knowledge better at follow-up, but not amongst all	Effective	Immediate!
Hölund[154]	14	N = 344 children	School	Monthly brushing instruction	Reduced levels of gingivitis	Effective intervention	1 month
Croft[52]	10	N = 780 children	School	Daily disclosure + brushing. Flossing for older children	No differences in gingivitis when compared with another school	Intervention not effective	Ongoing

Table 7.1. Quasi-experimental studies – sugar

Study	Quality score	Target population		Setting	Intervention	Results given	Conclusion	Follow-up	Mean intervention effect
Croucher et al.[164]	9	Children (pre-school) Expt Control	66 23	Community	Programme advising re snack choices plus various reinforcement techniques	Higher proportion of children chose safe snacks	Intervention effective	6 months	
Tan, Ruiter and Verhey[77]	9	Adults Expt Control	77 127	Workplace	DHE plus professional prophylaxis + group discussions	Reported consumption of sweet food and drinks lower in intervention group	Intervention affects reported behaviour	6 months	12% reduction in sweet food choices
Schou[78]	15	Adults Expt Control	68 68	Workplace	DHE to peer groups with 5 monthly repeat sessions	Greater belief in the preventive effect of good food choices	Intervention affects reported behaviour	3½ years	N/A
Milén et al.[148]	10	Children Expt Control	732 296	Clinic	Dental health advice provided at time of dental examination	Greater proportion of control group had high reported frequency of sugar consumption	Numbers too small for conclusive evidence	N/S	N/A

Table 7.2. Pre-/post- single group interventions – sugar

Study	Quality score	Target population	Setting	Intervention	Results given	Conclusion	Follow-up
Holm[152]	9	N = 4025 children	Clinics	Annual treatment plus OHI + DHE	No baseline data for snack choices	Inconclusive	Ongoing
Hargar and Krasse[165]	10	N = 135 adults	Workplace	DHE provided then participants taught colleagues	No. of individuals with high lactobacillus count reduced	Inconclusive	2 months

Appendix B. Methodology

General approach

In this review of health promotion interventions for providing oral health, the interpretation of the term 'oral health' was not limited simply to purely clinical measures. Non-clinical outcomes such as knowledge levels, oral health-related hygiene behaviours, oral health-related eating behaviours, attitudes and beliefs were also considered as outcomes which health promotion efforts aim to influence. Each component of interventions was examined in order that the effectiveness of the programme for each separate outcome could be determined. The interventions and their effectiveness are presented as tables for each outcome but summary conclusions are presented as text. Within the text, the validity of the measures used to assess outcomes is considered.

Given the wide range of methods, outcomes and setting within which oral health promotion takes place, the review is divided into chapters according to outcome measure and within each chapter different study designs are considered separately. The target group, setting and quality of the study are noted within the tables.

The aim was to produce a review which is scientifically defensible and free from bias. Achievement of that goal required a systematic approach to the information retrieved and reliable and valid methods of abstracting data. Finally a system for rating the quality of the information was deemed essential.

Methodological considerations in primary evaluative studies

The most convincing evidence about the effectiveness of an intervention comes from studies which test whether an exposed group has a different incidence of disease, or risk factor, from that of the general population. However, when reviewing such studies, a number of factors should be kept in mind.

The population in the study should be representative of the population with whom the intervention will be used, subsequent to testing. Many of the studies reviewed chose instead populations which were convenient or accessible and often, it would seem, there was no intention to apply the intervention more widely if it were successful.

Random allocation to study and control groups is considered to be a key factor in conducting reliable effectiveness studies. Firstly, randomisation eliminates selection bias on the part of the participants and the investigators. For example, if children were allocated by a dentist to test and control groups, he might (albeit subconsciously) tend to allocate children with higher disease rates to the treatment group if he believed that it might be beneficial. This would clearly distort the results. Secondly, randomisation helps to create groups which are similar in all factors which influence disease rates whether these are known or unknown. For example, allocation of children from one school to an intervention whilst using children from another school as controls might create a study in which test and control groups are radically different in socioeconomic status. Since socioeconomic status is associated with levels of caries and periodontal disease, such allocation procedures will distort the data. Finally, randomisation allows statistical analysis to be used on the data.

A further important consideration in studies of effectiveness is the potential bias introduced by the expectations of the investigator (and the participant). However, double-blind studies are often not feasible when assessing the effectiveness of oral health promotion interventions since, for example, it is impossible for a participant not to know that they have been taught toothbrushing. This issue is particularly important if the outcome is subjectively determined, for example, 'attitude to toothcleaning'.

Appendix C. Details of methodology of the review

1. Research question and hypothesis tested
The null hypothesis tested was:
Ho = Health promotion does not bring about an improvement in oral health.

Thus, the outcome measure upon which the review will rest is 'oral health'. The review did not, however, limit its interpretation of this outcome to purely clinical measures. Knowledge, attitudes, behaviour and self-reported behaviour were also considered as outcomes which oral health promotion sets out to achieve. The validity of the measures used to assess these outcomes was addressed as part of the review.

2. Search strategy
The search strategy had five stages:
1. Personal files were searched and a panel of ten 'experts' in the field were contacted to request that they do the same. Cooperating individuals were offered recompense for their time and expertise. Letters were also sent to members of relevant special interest groups and to postgraduate deans.

2. Computerised literature search of computer-stored databases. This was carried out by a medical librarian. The MeSH headings used by Schou and Locker and Health Promotion Wales were used but professional guidance from an expert indexer was also taken. The databases included MEDLINE, E.Med, CANCERLIT, Dissertation Abstracts Outline, government document listings, Current Research in Britain, Dental Abstracts, Health Service Abstracts.

3. The reference lists of the retrieved articles were reviewed for hitherto unretrieved papers.

4. Newly identified articles were reviewed for relevance.

5. All journals with material published in the subject area were handsearched and this followed an iterative process. In all, 96 journals were examined.

3. Assessing the relevance of the primary studies
Studies were included if published between 1980 and 1995 and if they were published in English or if an English abstract was available. Time constraints made translation unachievable.

Multiple published reports from the same study contributed only once to the review. The report which achieves the highest quality rating (see below) was selected for inclusion.

Studies which present incomplete data are analogous to drop-outs and non-respondents in clinical trials and were therefore included in the review.

4. Assessing the quality of the published reports

Each paper was 'scored' for quality. This quality score, plus the post-intervention follow-up period was reported for each paper. These items were taken into consideration in the qualitative synthesis of the results.

Data abstraction

Data abstraction forms were developed, pilot tested and revised as necessary. Abstracters were formally trained by the principal investigators and reliability of abstraction was assessed at the beginning of the study. A sample of papers was periodically abstracted by the investigators as part of ongoing quality control. The abstracters and the writers of the review were blinded to the publication details of the article.

5. Combining the evidence

Where possible, the results of studies were systematically combined using meta-analytic techniques, in order to give a quantitative estimate of the health-promoting effect of interventions. Narrative syntheses of groups of studies were written, taking into account the design, quality and follow-up period within the separate studies.

Exclusion criteria

Studies were excluded from the review if no measure of outcome was reported. Whilst this criterion meant that papers describing community actions or development of political pressure groups were excluded, this is considered appropriate given the target audience. The review focuses on oral health promotion initiatives and interventions which might form part of the purchaser–provider contract. Roles such as advocacy are purchaser responsibilities and are thus not contracted for. It was therefore considered pointless to include descriptive studies in the document.

6. Data abstraction and quality assessment

Each paper identified was classified by study design, the target population, the setting, outcome measure and the follow-up period. In addition, twenty items were used to determine the quality of the paper.

The quality score was ascertained by calculating the number of affirmative answers to the following questions.

Was the research goal clearly defined?
Was the intervention fully described for the intervention group?
Was the intervention fully described for the control group?
Was the study population clearly defined?

Was it stated how subjects were attained?
Were the subjects clearly defined?
Was the method of allocation, or similarity between groups described?
Were groups compared on any variables?
Were the outcome measures clearly defined?
Were the outcome measures objective?
Were the outcome measures tested for validity?
Were the outcome measures tested for reliability?
Were the outcome assessors blinded?
Were the participants blinded?
Was the statistical analysis appropriate?
Was the sample size for each group given?
Was there a sample size justification?
Was the statistical significance defined?
Was drop-out rate given?
Was drop-out rate < 10%?
Were drop-outs accounted for?

It can be seen that this schedule places particular weight on the definition, validity and reliability of the outcome measure and the drop-out rates, as well as scoring the articles for the general quality of the research design. Particular attention was paid to these two items for two reasons.

1. It is generally accepted that adequate randomisation, validity of outcome and drop-out rate are key criteria for determining the robustness of a study's design.

2. The purpose of this review requires that it identifies the types of intervention which can be recommended as effective with particular groups and settings. Thus, the outcome of interventions is of prime importance as is their acceptability to target populations.

The decision was made to assign a quality score as well as dividing the review according to study design. This allows well-conducted studies of less robust design to be accorded as much weight in the qualitative synthesis as poorly conducted studies of robust design.

Appendix D. Quality assessment form

1. ID No. _____

2. First author _____

3. Study design
      Randomised controlled trial ☐
      Quasi-experimental ☐
      Single group before–after ☐
      Multiple baseline across subjects/groups design ☐
      Case study ☐
      Mass media ☐

4. Was the research goal clearly defined?   Yes ☐
                                                     No ☐

      e.g.   CLEAR   'examined the effect of tooth-brushing instruction on periodontal loss'

             VAGUE   'assessed the effect of tooth-brushing on periodontal health'

5. Was the intervention

   (a)   fully described

           –   for the treatment group   Yes ☐
                                        No ☐

           –   for the control group   Yes ☐
                                        No ☐
                                        NA ☐

   (b)   educational only   Yes ☐
                                      No ☐

   (c)   planned to:
      change knowledge ☐
      change attitudes ☐
      change beliefs/values/intentions ☐
      change oral hygiene behaviour ☐

change use of service ☐
change sugar consumption ☐
alter plaque level ☐
prevent gingivitis/bleeding ☐
prevent periodontal disease ☐
prevent dental caries ☐

6. (a) Was the study population clearly defined, i.e.   Yes ☐
   were the in/exclusion criteria given?   No ☐

   (b) Was it stated how subjects were obtained?   Yes ☐
   (e.g. employees in an industrial firm selected at   No ☐
   random)

   (c) Were the subjects:

   children ☐
   elderly ☐
   people with handicap/disabilities ☐
   adults ☐
   ethnic minorities ☐

7. Was the setting:

   school ☐
   institution ☐
   dental practice ☐
   workplace ☐
   other ☐

8. (a) If RCT, was method of the allocation to groups   Yes ☐
   described?   No ☐

   (b) If quasi-experimental, was an attempt made to   Yes ☐
   achieve similarity of groups?   No ☐

   (c) Were groups compared on any of variables   Yes ☐
   e.g. gender, age, SES, . . .) to check similarity?   No ☐

9. Were the outcome measures:

   (a) clearly defined?   Yes ☐
     No ☐

   (b) objective?   Yes ☐
     No ☐

(c)	tested for validity and reliability?	Yes	☐
		No	☐

10. Was it stated whether outcome assessors were blinded as to intervention/control?

    Yes ☐
    No ☐
    NA ☐

11. Was it stated whether participants were blinded as to intervention/control?

    Yes ☐
    No ☐
    NA ☐

12. (a) Is the statistical analysis appropriate?

    Yes ☐
    No ☐

    (d) Was sample size for each group given?

    Yes ☐
    No ☐

    (e) Was there a sample size justification before the study?

    Yes ☐
    No ☐

    (f) Was statistical significance defined?

    Yes ☐
    No ☐

13. Were details of drop-outs given?

    Yes ☐
    No ☐

    If yes, was drop-out rate $\leq$ 10%
                            > 10%

14. Were drop-outs accounted for?

    Yes ☐
    No ☐

15. Was the follow-up period defined?

    Yes ☐
    No ☐

    If yes, tick follow-up period

    Immediate ☐
    < 2 weeks ☐
      2–4 weeks ☐
      5–8 weeks ☐
      9–12 weeks ☐
      13 weeks–6 months ☐
      6 months–1 year ☐
      1 year–2 years ☐
      2 years–5 years ☐
      5 years + ☐

References

1. Catford, J C and Nutbeam, D. Smoking in hospitals. *Lancet* 1983; ii (8341):94–6.

2. Downer, M. The improving health of United Kingdom adults and prospects for the future. *British Dental Journal* 1991; **170**:326.

3. Department of Health. *An oral health strategy for England.* Department of Health, 1994.

4. Reisine, S. Dental health and public policy: the social impact of dental disease. *American Journal of Public Health* 1985; **75**:27–30.

5. Reisine, S and Miller, J. A longitudinal study of work loss related to dental disease. *Social Science and Medicine* 1985; **21**:1309–14.

6. Shaw, W, Meek, S and Jones, D. Nicknames, teasing, harassment and the salience of dental features among school children. *British Journal of Orthodontics* 1980; **7**:75–80.

7. Smith, J and Sheiham, A. How dental conditions handicap the elderly. *Community Dentistry and Oral Epidemiology* 1979; **7**:305–10.

8. Health Committee 4th report (session 1992–93). *Dental services.* HMSO, 1993.

9. Horowitz, A M, Suomi, J D, Peterson, J K, Mathews, B L, Vogelsong, R H and Lyman, B A. Effects of supervised daily dental plaque removal by children after 3 years. *Community Dentistry and Oral Epidemiology* 1980; **8**:171–6.

10. Axelsson, P, Kristoffersson, K, Karlsson, R and Bratthal, D. A 30-month longitudinal study of the effects of some oral hygiene measures on streptococcus mutans and approximal dental caries. *Journal of Dental Research* 1987; **66**:761–5.

11. Craig, E W, Suckling, G W and Pearce, E I F. The effect of a preventive programme on dental plaque and caries in school children. *New Zealand Dental Journal* 1981; **77**:89–93.

12. Blinkhorn, A S and Wight, C. An assessment of two dental health education programmes for Scottish secondary school children. *Health Education Research* 1987; **2**(3):231–7.

13. Stiefel, D J, Rolla, R R and Truelove, E L. Effectiveness of various preventive methodologies for use with disabled persons. *Clinical Preventive Dentistry* 1984; **6**:17–22.

14. Holt, R D, Winter, G B, Fox, B, Askew, R, and Lo, G L. Dental health education through home visits to mothers with young children. *Community Dentistry and Oral Epidemiology* 1983; **11**:98–101.

15. Ekman, A and Persson, B. Effect of early dental health education for Finnish immigrant families. *Swedish Dental Journal* 1990; **14**:143–51.

16. Blount, R L and Stokes, T F. A comparison of the OHI-S and the PHP in an oral hygiene program. *Journal of Dentistry for Children* 1986; **53**:53–6.

17. Shein, B, Tsamtsouris, A and Rovero, J. Self-reported compliance and the effectiveness of prenatal dental education. *Journal of Clinical Paediatric Dentistry* 1991; **15**:102–8.

18. Axelsson, P and Lindhe, J. Effect of controlled oral hygiene procedures on caries and periodontal disease in adults: results after 6 years. *Journal of Clinical Periodontology* 1981; **8**:239–48.

19. Wight, C and Blinkhorn, A S. An assessment of two dental health education programmes for school children in the Lothian region of Scotland. *Journal of Paediatric Dentistry* 1988; **4**:1–7.

20. Fogels, H R, Cancro, L P, Bianco, J and Fischman, S L. The anticaries effect of supervised toothbrushing with a nonfluoride dentifrice. *Journal of Dentistry for Children* 1982; **49**:424–7.

21. Lalloo, R and Solanki, G S. An evaluation of a school-based comprehensive public oral health care programme. *Community Dental Health* 1994; **11**:152–5.

22. Kerebel, L-M, Le Cabellec, M-T, Kerebel, B and Daculsi, G. Effect of motivation on the oral health of French schoolchildren. *Journal of Dentistry for Children* 1985; **52**:287–92.

23. Rayner, J A. A dental health education programme, including home visits for nursery school children. *British Dental Journal* 1992; **172**:57–62.

24. Blinkhorn, A S, Taylor, I and Willcox, G F. Report of a dental health education programme in Bedfordshire. *British Dental Journal* 1981; **150**:319–22.

25. Blinkhorn, A S, Wight, C and Yardley, A. Report of two dental health programmes for adolescents in the Lothian region of Scotland. *Journal of Dentistry* 1987; **15**:213–17.

26. Olsen, C B, Brown, D F and Wright, F A C. Dental health promotion in a group of children at high risk of dental disease. *Community Dentistry and Oral Epidemiology* 1986; **14**:302–5.

27. Truin, G J, Plasschaert, A J M, König, K G and Vogels, A L M. Dental caries in 5-, 7-, 9- and 11-year-old schoolchildren during a 9-year dental health campaign in The Hague. *Community Dentistry and Oral Epidemiology* 1981; **9**:55–60.

28. Mann, J, Wolnerman, J S, Carlin, Y, Meir, S and Garfunkel, A A. The effect of dental education and dental treatment on the dental status of a handicapped population: a longitudinal study. *Special Care in Dentistry* 1986; **6**:180–1.

29. Petersen, P E. Evaluation of a dental preventive program for Danish chocolate workers. *Community Dentistry and Oral Epidemiology* 1989; **17**:53–9.

30. Ambjörnsen, E and Rise, J. The effect of verbal information and demonstration on denture hygiene in elderly people. *Acta Odontologica Scandinavica* 1985; **43**:19–24.

31. Baab, D A and Weinstein, P. Oral hygiene instruction using a self-inspection plaque index. *Community Dentistry and Oral Epidemiology* 1983; **11**:174–9.

32. Holt, R D, Winter, G B, Fox, B and Askew, R. Second assessment of London children involved in a scheme of dental health education in infancy. *Community Dentistry and Oral Epidemiology* 1989; **17**:180–2.

33. Horowitz, L G. Dental patient education: self-care to human health development. *Patient Education and Counseling* 1990; **15**:65–71.

34. Hetland, L, Midtun, N and Kristoffersen, T. Effect of oral hygiene instructions given by paraprofessional personnel. *Community Dentistry and Oral Epidemiology* 1981; **10**:8–14.

35. Bickley, S R, Shaw, L and Shaw, M J. The use and effect of clinical photographic records on the motivation and oral hygiene practices of a group of mentally handicapped adults. *Dental Health* 1990; **29**:3–5.

36. Tedesco, L A, Keffer, M A, Davis, E L and Christersson, L A. Effect of a social cognitive intervention on oral health status, behavior reports, and cognitions. *Journal of Periodontology* 1992; **63**:567–75.

37. Alcouffe, F. 'Spontaneous' oral hygiene: a predictor of future preventive behavior? *Community Dentistry and Oral Epidemiology* 1989; **17**:120–2.

38. Dowey, J A. Computer games for dental health education in primary schools. *Health Education* 1987; **46**:107–8.

39. Söderholm, G, Nobréis, N, Attström, R and Egelberg, J. Teaching plaque control, I: A five-visit versus a two-visit program. *Journal of Clinical Periodontology* 1982; **9**:203–13.

40. Albandar, J M, Buischi, Y A P, Mayer, M P A, and Axelsson, P. Long-term effect of two preventive programs on the incidence of plaque and gingivitis in adolescents. *Journal of Periodontology* 1994; **65**:605–10.

41. Lee, A J. Daily, dry toothbrushing in kindergarten. *Journal of School Health* 1980; **50**:506–9.

42. Knazan, Y L. Application of PRECEDE to dental health promotion for a Canadian well-elderly population. *Gerodontics* 1986; **2**:180–5.

43. Bullen, C, Rubenstein, L, Saravia, M E and Mourino, A P. Improving children's oral hygiene through parental involvement. *Journal of Dentistry for Children* 1988; **55**:125–8.

44. Bowen, D M. Effectiveness of the phase contrast microscope. *Dental Hygiene* 1981; **4**:26–30.

45. McCaul, K D, Glasgow, R E and O'Neill, H K. The problem of creating habits: establishing health-protective dental behaviors. *Health Psychology* 1992; **11**(2):101–10.

46. Stewart, J E, Jacobs-Schoen, M, Padilla, M R, Maeder, L A, Wolfe, G R and Hartz, G W. The effect of a cognitive behavioral intervention on oral hygiene. *Journal of Clinical Periodontology* 1991; **18**:219–22.

47. Boyd, R L. Longitudinal evaluation of a system for self-monitoring plaque control effectiveness in orthodontic patients. *Journal of Clinical Periodontology* 1983; **10**:380–8.

48. Glavind, L, Zeuner, E and Attström, R. Oral cleanliness and gingival health following oral hygiene instruction by self-educational programs. *Journal of Clinical Periodontology* 1984; **11**: 262–73.

49. Yeung, S C H, Howell, S and Fahey, P. Oral hygiene program for orthodontic patients. *American Journal of Orthodontics and Dentofacial Orthopedics* 1989; **96**:208–13.

50. Price, S and Kiyak, H A. A behavioral approach to improving oral health among the elderly. *Special Care in Dentistry* 1981; **1**:267–74.

51. Klass, K and Rhoden, C. Aspects of dental health education for preschool children and their parents. *Journal of Dentistry for Children* 1981; **48**:357–63.

52. Croft, L K. The effectiveness of the Toothkeeper Program after six years. *Texas Dental Journal* 1980; **9**:6–8.

53. Croucher, R E, Rodgers, A I, Franklin, R A J and Craft, M H. Results and issues arising from an evaluation of community dental health education: the case of the 'good teeth programme'. *Community Dental Health* 1985; **2**:89–97.

54. Davis, B and Costanzo, G. A comparison of the effectiveness of television vs live instruction for teaching flossing in the classroom. *Canadian Dental Hygienist* 1982; **16**:12–15.

55. Murray, J A and Epstein, L H. Improving oral hygiene with videotape modeling. *Behavior Modification* 1981; **5**:360–71.

56. Kiyak, H A and Mulligan, K. Studies of the relationship between oral health and psychological well-being. *Gerodontics* 1987; **3**:109–12.

57. Schwarz, E. Longitudinal evaluation of a preventive program provided by general dental practitioners to young adult Danes. *Community Dentistry and Oral Epidemiology* 1981; **9**:280–4.

58. Craft, M, Croucher, R and Dickinson, J. Preventive dental health in adolescents: short and long term pupil response to trials of an integrated curriculum package. *Community Dentistry and Oral Epidemiology* 1981; **9**:199–206.

59. Ivanovic, M and Lekic, P. Effect of a short-term educational programme without prophylaxis on control of plaque and gingival inflammation in school children. *Acta Stomatologica Croatica* 1990; **24**:123–31.

60. Melsen, B and Agerbaek, N. Effect of an instructional motivation program on oral health in Danish adolescents after 1 and 2 years. *Community Dentistry and Oral Epidemiology* 1980; **8**:72–8.

61. Ehudin, H E and Martin, H B. Tooth-tutoring: a pilot study to evaluate peer-teaching effectiveness. *Journal of Dentistry for Children* 1983; **50**:287–91.

62. McGlynn, F D, LeCompte, E J, Thomas, R G, Couts, F J and Melamed, B G. Effects of behavioral self-management on oral hygiene adherence among orthodontic patients. *American Journal of Orthodontics and Dentofacial Orthopedics* 1987; **91**:15–21.

63. Glavind, L, Zeuner, E and Attström, R. Oral hygiene instruction of adults by means of a self-instructional manual. *Journal of Clinical Periodontology* 1981; **8**:165–76.

64. Glavind, L, Christensen, H, Pedersen, E, Rosendahl, H and Amstrom, R. Oral health hygiene instruction in general dental practice by means of self-teaching manuals. *Journal of Clinical Periodontology* 1985; **12**:27–34.

65. Scruggs, R R, Warren, D P and Levine, P. Juvenile diabetics' oral health and locus of control: a pilot study. *Journal of Dental Hygiene* 1989; **63**:376–81.

66. Schou, L, Wight, C, Clemson, N, Douglas, S and Clark, C. Oral health promotion for institutionalised elderly. *Community Dentistry and Oral Epidemiology* 1989; **17**:2–6.

67. McGuire, M K, Sydney, S B, Zink, F J, Weber, M B and Fritz, M E. Evaluation of an oral disease control program administered to a clinic population at a suburban dental school. *Journal of Periodontology* 1980; **3**:607–13.

68. Shaw, M J and Shaw, L. The effectiveness of differing dental health education programmes in improving the oral health of adults with mental handicaps attending Birmingham adult training centres. *Community Dental Health* 1991; **8**:139–45.

69. Craft, M, Croucher, R, Dickinson, J, James, M, Clements, M and Rodgers, A-I. Natural Nashers: a programme of dental health education for adolescents in schools. *International Dental Journal* 1984; **34**: 204–13.

70. Söderholm, G and Egelberg, J. Teaching plaque control, II: 30-minute versus 15-minute appointments in a three-visit program. *Journal of Clinical Periodontology* 1982; **9**:214–22.

71. Torpaz, E, Noam, Y, Anaise, J Z and Sgan-Cohen, H. Effectiveness of dental health educational programs on oral cleanliness of schoolchildren in Israel. *Dental Hygiene* 1984; **12**:169–73.

72. Emier, B F, Windchy, A M, Zaino, S W, Feldman, S M and Scheetz, J P. The value of repetition and reinforcement in improving oral hygiene performance. *Journal of Periodontology* 1980; **2**:228–34.

73. Julien, M G. The effect of behaviour modification techniques on oral hygiene and gingival health of 10-year-old Canadian children. *International Journal of Paediatric Dentistry* 1994; **4**:3–11.

74. Gisselsson, H, Björn, A-L and Birkhed, D. Immediate and prolonged effect of individual preventive measures in caries and gingivitis susceptible children. *Swedish Dental Journal* 1983; **7**:13–21.

75. Houle, B A. The impact of long-term dental health education on oral hygiene behavior. *Journal of School Health* 1982; **52**:256–61.

76. Cutress, T W, Powell, R N, Kilisimasi, S, Tomiki, S and Holborow, D. A 3-year community-based periodontal disease prevention programme for adults in a developing nation. *International Dental Journal* 1991; **41**:323–34.

77. Tan, H H, Ruiter, E and Verhey, H. Effect of repeated dental health care education on gingival health, knowledge, attitude, behavior and perception. *Community Dentistry and Oral Epidemiology* 1981; **9**:15–21.

78. Schou, L. Active-involvement principle in dental health education. *Community Dentistry and Oral Epidemiology* 1985; **13**:128–32.

79. Hodge, H, Buchanan, M, O'Donnell, P, Topping, B and Banks, I. The evaluation of the junior dental health education programme developed in Sefton, England. *Community Dental Health* 1987; **4**:223–9.

80. Craft, M, Croucher, R and Blinkhorn, A. 'Natural Nashers' dental health education programme: the results of a field trial in Scotland. *British Dental Journal* 1984; **156**:103–5.

81. Arnold, C and Doyle, A J. Evaluation of the dental health education programme 'Natural Nashers'. *Community Dental Health* 1984; **1**:141–7.

82. Goodkind, R J, Loupe, M J, Clay, D J and DiAngelis, A J. Modifying the knowledge, skills and habits of denture patients. *Gerodontics* 1988; **4**:95–100.

83. Wright, I G and Pack, A R C. Evaluation of a dental health educational project in the classroom. *New Zealand Dental Journal* 1979; **75**:15–19.

84. Wright, F A C. An assessment of dental health education. *New Zealand Dental Journal* 1984; **80**:74–80.

85. Sutcliffe, P, Rayner, J A and Brown, M D. Daily supervised toothbrushing in nursery schools. *British Dental Journal* 1984; **157**:201–4.

86. Hölund, U. The effect of a nutrition education programme 'learning by teaching' on the dietary attitudes of a group of adolescents. *Community Dental Health* 1990; **7**:395–401.

87. Cohen, S, Sarnat, H and Shalgi, G. The role of instruction and a brushing device on the oral hygiene of blind children. *Clinical Preventive Dentistry* 1991; **13**:8–12.

88. Scanlan, S E. Applying the Good Teeth Programme. *Health Education Journal* 1988; **47**:2–3.

89. Lundstrom, F and Hamp, S-E. Effect of oral hygiene education on children with or without subsequent orthodontic treatment. *Scandinavian Journal of Dental Research* 1980; **88**:53–9.

90. Bergstrom, J. Oral hygiene compliance and gingivitis expression in cigarette smokers. *Scandinavian Journal of Dental Research* 1990; **98**:497–503.

91. Bader, J D, Rozier, R G, McFall, W T, Sams, D H, Graves, R C, Slome, B A and Ramsey, D L. Evaluating and influencing periodontal diagnostic and treatment behaviors in general practice. *American Dental Association Journal* 1990; **121**:720–4.

92. Odman, P A, Lange, A L and Bakdash, M B. Utilisation of locus of control in the prediction of patients' oral hygiene performance. *Journal of Clinical Periodontology* 1984; **11**:367–72.

93. Messer, J G. The Nain THETA programme: a peer group dental education program. *Canadian Journal of Community Dentistry* 1987; **2**:18–21.

94. Heasman, P A, Jacobs, D J and Chapple, I L. An evaluation of the effectiveness and patient compliance with plaque control methods in the prevention of periodontal disease. *Clinical Preventive Dentistry* 1989; **11**:24–8.

95. Brown, R H, Morilleau, J and Cross, P. A toothbrushing programme in a school for the intellectually handicapped. *New Zealand Dental Journal* 1980; **76**:21–2.

96. Jodaikin, A. The effect of oral health care instruction during the 1979 National Dental Health Week on plaque removal by school children. *Dental Association of South Africa Journal* 1981; **36**:691–3.

97. Towner, E M L. The 'Gleam Team' programme: development and evaluation of a dental health education package for infant schools. *Community Dental Health* 1984; **1**:181–91.

98. Simmons, S, Smith, R and Gelbier, S. Effect of oral hygiene instruction on brushing skills in preschool children. *Community Dentistry and Oral Epidemiology* 1983; **11**:193–8.

99. Schou, L, Wight, C and Wohlgemuth, B. Deprivation and dental health: the benefits of a child dental health campaign in relation to deprivation as estimated by the uptake of free meals at school. *Community Dental Health* 1991; **8**:147–54.

100. Rich, S K, Friedman, J-A and Schultz, L A. Effects of flossing on plaque and gingivitis in third grade schoolchildren. *Journal of Public Health Dentistry* 1989; **49**:73–7.

101. Weinstein, P, Milgrom, P, Meinick, S, Beach, B and Spadafora, A. How effective is oral hygiene instruction? Results after 6 and 24 weeks. *Journal of Public Health Dentistry* 1989; **49**:32–8.

102. Petersen, P E and Nörtov, B. Evaluation of a dental public health programme for old-age pensioners in Denmark. *Journal of Public Health Dentistry* 1994; **54**:73–9.

103. Honkala, E, Karvonen, S, Rimpela, A, Rajala, M, Rimpela, M and Prattala, R. Oral health promotion among Finnish adolescents between 1977 and 1989. *Health Promotion International* 1991; **6**(1):21–30.

104. Benitez, C, O'Sullivan, D and Tinanoff, N. Effect of a preventive approach for the treatment of nursing bottle caries. *Journal of Dentistry for Children* 1994; **61**:46–9.

105. Smorang, J and Erikson, J. An extended care facility: Mouthcare project – CFDE report. *Probe* 1994; **28**: 18–20.

106. Thomas, J. A multidisciplinary approach to health promotion for seniors. *Canadian Dental Hygienist* 1992; **26**:29–31.

107. Weisenberg, M, Kegeles, S S and Lund, A K. Children's health beliefs and acceptance of a dental preventive activity. *Journal of Health and Social Behavior* 1980; **21**:59–74.

108. Blount, R L and Stokes, T F. Contingent public posting of photographs to reinforce dental hygiene. *Behavior Modification* 1984; **8**:79–92.

109. Claerhout, S and Lutzker, J R. Increasing children's self-initiated compliance to dental regimens. *Behaviour Therapy* 1981; **12**:165–76.

110. Dahlquist, L M, Gil, K M, Hodges, J, Kalfus, G R, Ginsberg, A and Holborn, S. The effects of behavioural intervention on dental flossing skills in children. *Journal of Pediatric Psychology* 1985; **10**:403–12.

111. Swan, J J, Allard, G B and Holborn, S W. The Good Toothbrushing Game: a school based dental hygiene program for increasing the toothbrushing effectiveness of children. *Journal of Applied Behavior Analysis* 1982; **15**:171–6.

112. Dahlquist, L M and Gil, K M. Using parents to maintain improved dental flossing skills in children. *Journal of Applied Behavior Analysis* 1986; **19**:255–60.

113. Poche, C, McCubbrey, H and Munn, T. The development of correct toothbrushing technique in pre-school children. *Journal of Applied Behavior Analysis* 1982; **15**:315–20.

114. Weinstein, P, Milgrom, P, Meinick, S, Beach, B and Spadafora, A. How effective is oral hygiene instruction? Results after 6 and 24 weeks. *Journal of Public Health Dentistry* 1989; **49**:32–8.

115. Baab, D and Weinstein, P. Longitudinal evaluation of a self-inspection plaque index in periodontal recall patients. *Journal of Clinical Periodontology* 1986; **13**:313–18.

116. Tedesco, L A, Keffer, M A and Davis, E L. Social cognitive theory and relapse prevention: reframing patient compliance. *Journal of Dental Education* 1991; **55**:575–81.

117. Albandar, J M, Buischi, Y A P, Oliveira, L B and Axelsson, P. Lack of effect of oral hygiene training on periodontal disease progression over 3 years in adolescents. *Journal of Periodontology* 1995; **66**:255–60.

118. Feaver, G and Galgut, P. A pilot study into factors affecting the efficacy of two different plaque control programmes in relation to reduction in plaque and gingivitis levels in young adults. *Journal of Dental Health* 1985; **24**:3–4.

119. Glavind, L, Zeuner, E and Attström, R. Evaluation of various feedback mechanisms in relation to compliance by adult patients with oral home care instructions. *Journal of Clinical Periodontology* 1983; **10**:57–68.

120. Cutress, T W, Powell, R N, Kilisimasi, S, Tomiki, S and Holborow, D. A three year community-based periodontal disease prevention programme for adults in a developing nation. *International Dental Journal* 1991; **41**:323–34.

121. Kallio, P and Ainamo, J. Self-assessment of gingival bleeding. *International Dental Journal* 1990; **40**:231–6.

122. Zimmerman, M, Bornstein, R and Martinsson, T. Simplified preventive dentistry program for Chilean refugees: effectiveness of one versus two instructional sessions. *Community Dentistry and Oral Epidemiology* 1993; **21**:143–7.

123. Schou, L and Wight, C. Does dental health education affect inequalities in dental health? *Community Dental Health* 1993; **11**:97–100.

124. Takahashi, Y, Kamijyo, H, Kawanishi, S and Takaesu, Y. The effects of ultrasonic scaling with oral hygiene education on the distribution of pathological pockets using CPITN diagnostic standards. *Community Dental Health* 1989; **6**:31–7.

125. Glassman, P, Miller, C, Wozniak, T and Jones, C. A preventive dentistry training program for caretakers of persons with disabilities residing in community residential facilities. *Special Care in Dentistry* 1994; **14**:137–43.

126. Nikias, M K, Budner, N S and Breakstone, R S. Maintenance of oral home care preventive practices: an empirical study in two dental settings. *Journal of Public Health Dentistry* 1982; **42**:7–28.

127. Tenenbaum, H. Impact of a periodontal course on oral hygiene and gingival health among senior dental students. *Community Dentistry and Oral Epidemiology* 1980; **8**:335–8.

128. Hartshorne, J E, Carstens, I L, Beilinsohn, B and Potgieter, G. The effectiveness of a school-based oral health education program – a pilot study. *Dental Association of South Africa Journal* 1989; **44**:5–10.

129. Moltzer, G and Hoogstraten, J. The effect of three methods of dental health care instruction and dental knowledge, attitude, behaviour and fear. *Community Dental Health* 1986; **3**:83–9.

130. Hoogstraten, J and Moltzer, G. Effects of dental health care instruction on knowledge, attitude, behavior and fear. *Community Dentistry and Oral Epidemiology* 1983; **11**:278–82.

131. Rantanen, T, Siirilä, HS and Lehvilä, P. Effect of instruction and motivation on dental knowledge and behavior among wearers of partial dentures. *Acta Odontologica Scandinavica* 1980; **38**:9–15.

132. Malvitz, D M and Broderick, E B. Assessment of a dental disease prevention program after three years. *Journal of Public Health Dentistry* 1989; **49**:54–8.

133. Alcouff, F. Improvement of oral hygiene habits: a psychological approach: 2-year data. *Journal of Clinical Periodontology* 1988; **15**:617–20.

134. Dulac, M H, Ivory, J and Horowitz, A M. Working with non-dental groups to influence adoption of self-applied fluoride programs in schools: one approach. *Journal of School Health* 1983; **53**:184–8.

135. Uitenbroek, D G, Schaub, R M H, Tromp, J A H and Kant, J H. Dental hygienists' influence on the patients' knowledge, motivation, self-care and perception of change. *Community Dentistry and Oral Epidemiology* 1989; **17**:87–90.

136. Peterson, F L Jr and Rubinson, L. An evaluation of the effects of the American Dental Association's dental health education program on the knowledge, attitudes and health locus of control of high school students. *Journal of School Health* 1982; **52**:63–9.

137. ter Horst, G and Hoogstraten, J. Immediate and delayed effects of a dental health education film on periodontal knowledge, attitudes and reported behavior of Dutch adolescents. *Community Dentistry and Oral Epidemiology* 1989; **17**:123–6.

138. Lachapelle, D, Desaulniers, G and Bujold, N. Dental health education for adolescents: assessing attitude and knowledge following two educational approaches. *Canadian Journal of Public Health* 1989; **80**:339–44.

139. Laiho, M, Honkala, E, Nyssonen, V and Milén, A. Three methods of oral health education in secondary schools. *Scandinavian Journal of Dental Research* 1993; **101**:422–7.

140. Søgaard, A J and Holst, D. The effect of different school-based dental health education programmes in Norway. *Community Dental Health* 1988; **5**:169–84.

141. Walsh, M M. Effects of school-based dental health education on knowledge, attitudes and behavior of adolescents in San Francisco. *Community Dentistry and Oral Epidemiology* 1985; **13**:133–5.

142. Goepferd, S J. An infant oral health program: the first 18 months. *Pediatric Dentistry* 1987; **9**:8–12.

143. Hölund, U. Effect of a nutrition education programme, 'Learning by teaching', on adolescents' knowledge and beliefs. *Community Dentistry and Oral Epidemiology* 1990; **18**:61–5.

144. Søgaard, A J, Tuominen, R, Holst, D and Gjermo, P. The effect of 2 teaching programs on the gingival health of 15-year-old schoolchildren. *Journal of Clinical Periodontology* 1987; **14**:165–70.

145. Kleinman, S P. Development of dental health knowledge tests for the primary grades. *Health Education* 1981; **12**:16–19.

146. Barrie, R B and Carstens, I L. An evaluation of school dental health education programmes. *Dental Association of South Africa Journal* 1989; **43**:137–40.

147. Russell, B A, Horowitz, A M and Frazier, P J. School-based preventive regimens and oral health knowledge and practices of sixth graders. *Journal of Public Health Dentistry* 1989; **49**:192–200.

148. Milén, A, Hausen, H, Tala, H and Heinonen, O P. Dental health habits among pre-school nonparticipants in public dental care. *Community Dental Health* 1985; **2**:109–14.

149. McIntyre, J, Wight, C and Blinkhorn, A S. A reassessment of Lothian Health Board's dental health education programme for primary school children. *Community Dental Health* 1985; **2**:99–108.

150. Walsh, M M, Heckman, B H and Moreau-Diettinger, R. Use of gingival bleeding for reinforcement of oral home care behavior. *Community Dentistry and Oral Epidemiology* 1985; **13**:133–5.

151. Robinson, L and Tappe, M. An evaluation of a preschool dental health program. *Journal of Dentistry for Children* 1987; **54**:186–92.

152. Holm, A-K. Education and diet in the prevention of caries in the preschool child. *Journal of Dentistry* 1990; **18**:308–14.

153. Peterson, F L and Rubinson, L. An evaluation of a school dental health program: phase I. *Journal of Dentistry for Children* 1981; **4**:433–6.

154. Hölund, U. Promoting change of adolescents' sugar consumption: the 'Learning by teaching' study. *Health Education and Research* 1990; **5**:451–8.

155. Blinkhorn, A S, Downer, M C, Mackie, I C and Bleasdale, R S. Evaluation of a practice based preventive programme for adolescents. *Community Dentistry and Oral Epidemiology* 1981; **9**:275–9.

156. Fuller, S S and Harding, M. The use of the sugar clock in dental health education. *British Dental Journal* 1991; **170**:414–16.

157. Galgut, P N, Waite, I M, Todd-Pokropek, A and Barnby, G J. The relationship between the multidimensional health locus of control and the performance of subjects on a preventive periodontal programme. *Journal of Clinical Periodontology* 1987; **14**:171–5.

158. Kegeles, S S and Lund, A K. Adolescents' health beliefs and acceptance of a novel preventive dental activity: replication and extension. *Health Education Quarterly* 1982; **9**(2 & 3):192–209.

159. Maruyama, S and Koyazu, T. Effect of dental drawings and colouring on attitudes of child patients. *Journal of Dentistry for Children* 1988; **55**:129–32.

160. Wikner, S. An attempt to motivate improved sugar discipline in a 12-year-old high caries-risks group. *Community Dentistry and Oral Epidemiology* 1986; **14**:5–7.

161. Zimmerman, M, Bornstein, R and Martinsson, T. Attitudes and knowledge about preventive dental care in Chilean refugees in Sweden. *Community Dental Health* 1993; **10**:343–51.

162. Byrd-Bredbenner, C, O'Connell, L H, Shannon, B and Eddy, J M. A nutrition curriculum for health education: its effect on students' knowledge, attitude and behavior. *Journal of School Health* 1984; **54**:385–8.

163. Mackie, I C, Worthington, H V and Hobson, P. An investigation into sugar-containing and sugar-free over-the-counter medicines stocked and recommended by pharmacists in the North Western Region of England. *British Dental Journal* 1983; **175**:93–8.

164. Croucher, R, Rodgers, A I, Humpherson, W A and Crush, L. The 'spread of effect' of a school based dental health education project. *Community Dentistry and Oral Epidemiology* 1985; **13**:205–7.

165. Harger, B and Krasse, B. Dental health education by 'barefoot doctors'. *Community Dentistry and Oral Epidemiology* 1983; **11**:333–6.

166. Bohannan, H M, Klein, S P, Disney, J A, Bell, R M, Graves, R C and Foch, C B. A summary of the results of the national Preventive Dentistry Demonstration Program. *Canadian Dental Association Journal* 1985; **6**: 435–41.

167. Sakai, O and Horii, K-I. Spreading the effect of caries prevention by community organisation in schoolchildren in Japan. *Journal of Dental Research* 1980; **59**DII:2226–32.

168. Karjalainen, S, Le Bell, Y and Karhuvaara, L. Salivary parameters and efficiency of dietary instructions to reduce sugar intake among 7–8 year-old schoolchildren. *Scandinavian Journal of Dental Research* 1988; **96**:22–9.

169. Kohler, B, Andreen, I, Jonsson, B and Hultqvist, E. Effect of caries preventive measures on streptococcus mutans and lactobacilli in selected mothers. *Scandinavian Journal of Dental Research* 1982; **90**:102–8.

170. Bakdash, M B, Lange, A L and McMillan, D G. The effect of a televised periodontal campaign on public periodontal awareness. *Journal of Periodontology* 1983; **7**:666–70.

171. Bakdash, M B, McMillan, D G and Lange, A L. Minnesota Periodontal Awareness Television Campaign. *North West Dentistry* 1984; **6**:12–17.

172. Bian, J Y, Zhang, B X and Rong, W S. Evaluating the social impact and effectiveness of the four-year 'Love Teeth Day' campaign in China. *Advances in Dental Research* 1995; **9**:130–3.

173. Murtomaa, H and Masalin, K. Effects of a national dental health campaign in Finland. *Acta Odontologica Scandinavica* 1984; **42**: 297–303.

174. Søgaard, A J. The effect of a mass-media dental health education campaign. *Health Education Research* 1988; **3**(3):243–55.

175. Rise, J and Søgaard, A J. Effect of a mass media periodontal campaign upon preventive knowledge and behavior in Norway. *Community Dentistry and Oral Epidemiology* 1988; **16**:1–4.

176. Schou, L. Use of mass media and active involvement in a national dental health campaign in Scotland. *Community Dentistry and Oral Epidemiology* 1987; **15**:14–18.

177. Whittle, J G, Pitkethly, D and Wilson, M C. A dental health promotion campaign in a shopping centre. *Health Education Research* 1994; **9**:261–5.

178. Schou, L and Locker, D. *Oral health: a review of the effectiveness of health education and health promotion.* Utrecht: Dutch Centre for Health Promotion and Health Education, 1994.

179. Kuthy, R A and Durkee, J. Education: a key to fluoridation compliance. *Journal of Public Health Dentistry* 1985; **45**:247–54.

180. Smith, K G and Christen, K A. A fluoridation campaign: the Phoenix experience. *Journal of Public Health Dentistry* 1990; **50**:319–23.

181. Lee, J. The reorganisation of the city of Toronto dental services: a community development model. *Journal of Public Health Dentistry* 1991; **51**:99–102.

182. Kay, E J and Locker, D. Is dental health education effective? A systematic review of current evidence. *Community Dentistry and Oral Epidemiology* 1996; **24**:231–5.

183. Sprod, A J, Anderson, R and Treasure, E T. *Effective oral health promotion: literature review.* Technical Report No. 20. Cardiff: Health Promotion Wales, 1996.

184. Brown, L F. Research in dental health education and health promotion: a review of the literature. *Health Education Quarterly* 1994; **21**:83–102.